YoungWriters 2005 POE

PLAYGROU

Let your creativity flow...

ode
limerick haiku
rhyme
balla

Bristol
Edited by Steve Twelvetree

 Young**Writers**

First published in Great Britain in 2005 by:
Young Writers
Remus House
Coltsfoot Drive
Peterborough
PE2 9JX
Telephone: 01733 890066
Website: www.youngwriters.co.uk

SB ISBN 1 84602 118 9

Foreword

Young Writers was established in 1991 and has been passionately devoted to the promotion of reading and writing in children and young adults ever since. The quest continues today. Young Writers remains as committed to the fostering of burgeoning poetic and literary talent as ever.

This year's Young Writers competition has proven as vibrant and dynamic as ever and we are delighted to present a showcase of the best poetry from across the UK. Each poem has been carefully selected from a wealth of *Playground Poets* entries before ultimately being published in this, our thirteenth primary school poetry series.

Once again, we have been supremely impressed by the overall high quality of the entries we have received. The imagination, energy and creativity which has gone into each young writer's entry made choosing the best poems a challenging and often difficult but ultimately hugely rewarding task - the general high standard of the work submitted amply vindicating this opportunity to bring their poetry to a larger appreciative audience.

We sincerely hope you are pleased with our final selection and that you will enjoy *Playground Poets Bristol* for many years to come.

Contents

Name	Page
Aman Singh (9)	17
Shuayb Mahood (9)	17
Sean Crawford (9)	18
Ethan Evans (9)	18
Alastair Monk (9)	18
Charlie Williams (9)	19
Oliver Dann (9)	19
Nuala Keohane (8)	19
Joe Widdecombe (9)	20
Christopher Sainsbury (8)	20
Megan Lockhart (8)	21
Elie Ben-Shlomo (8)	21
Katerina Nicholson (8)	22
Ella Voke (9)	22
Anna Soffe (7)	22
Laura Lane (8)	23
Sally Best (8)	23
Harry Magill (9)	23
Grace McNamara (8)	24
Franklin Taylor Moore (9)	25
Charlie Taylor (8)	25
Anna Murphy (9)	26
Annie Rolt (9)	27
Cristina Sved-Dures (9)	28
Anna Bunting (8)	28
Guy Remmers (9)	28
Lara Coode (7)	29
Elizabeth Vise (7)	29
Katie Barrett Powell (7)	29
Suki Penrose Britton (9)	30
Mehreen Siddique (8)	30
Lawrence Pryn (9)	31
Luke Stafford (9)	31
Natasha Simmons (9)	32
Tom Bentley (7)	32
Baisha Copeman (9)	33
Umay Habiba Zaman (8)	33
Katy Ruck (8)	34
Karis Hodgson (9)	34
Georgey Stuart-Mullin (9)	35
Jan Monks (8)	35
Rosalind Barnett (9)	35

Maddy Tickell (8)	36
Charlotte Fry (7)	36
Isabelle Fenner (9)	36
Ansaar Malik (9)	37
Dougie Murdoch (8)	37
Cara Vaitilingam (7)	38
Gus Lloyd (9)	38
Rebekah Overton (10)	39
Melissa Ward (7)	39
Jim Ratcliffe (9)	39
Jack Redpath (9)	40
Evie Smithson (9)	40
Florence Gregory (10)	41
Emily Stewart-Reid (8)	42
James Crawford (7)	42
Alasdair Marchant (10)	42
Cherry Stewart-Czerkas (10)	43
Rose Baker (7)	43
Genevieve Alsop (8)	44
Patrick Collings (7)	44
Isaac Harbord (10)	44

Cherry Garden Primary School

Elizabeth Illing (11)	45
George Yates (11)	46
Hannah Powell (10)	46
Jonathan Dick (10)	47
Holly Adams (10)	48
Sophie Boulton (10)	49
Ben Filer (11)	49
Alex Smith (10)	50
Harrison Guy (10)	50
James Smith (11)	51
Elliot Cumming (10)	52
Abi Denham (11)	52
Georgia Cousins (10)	53
Adam Ring (10)	53
Alex Sellars (11)	54
Paul Nicholls (10)	54
Kane Fews (10)	55
Stephen Andrews (11)	55

Harry Ball (8)	75
Matthew Davies (8)	75
Leon Worthington (8)	75
Jack Digby (9)	76
Harry Pincott (8)	76
Charlotte Attwood (7)	76
James Robinson (8)	77
Lily Allen (9)	77
Cyrus Caven (10)	78
Sam Crew (11)	78
Amy-Ruth Spreadbury (11)	79
Jonathan Lowrie (11)	79
Philip Roy Box (11)	80
Jessica Derrick (10)	80
Emma Fredericks (11)	81
Joshua Wanklyn (8)	81
Callum Braley (10)	82
Alex Wakley (10)	82
Alex Knight (9)	83
Nathan Rennolds (7)	83
Jemma Kinsey (10)	83
Calvin Peters (10)	84
Kirby Malone (10)	84
Cameron Nichols (9)	84
Jack Pitt (10)	85
David Roberts (8)	85
Adam Henry Rivers (10)	86

Holymead Junior School

Jessica Silman (10)	86
Abbie Rose Cliff (10)	87
Laura Perry (10)	87
Sabina Porter (10)	88
Graciela Berrios- Silva (11)	88
Jack Chianese (11)	89
Jordan Cross (10)	89
Alex Buss (11)	90
Grace Gibbs (11)	91
Emma Francis (10)	91
Amie Collett (11)	91
Luke Addison (10)	92

James Nichol (11)   92
Faith Evans (10)   93
Samantha Mogg (11)   93
Taylor Bragg (11)   94
Laura Wood (10)   94
Gabriella Aimee Cotton (11)   95
Maddie Austin (10)   95
Alex Kelly (11)   96
Jade Lewin (11)   96
Sam Iles (11)   97
Anna Yeatman (10)   97
Elliot Mills   98
Natasha Joslin (11)   98

North Road CP School

Alice Riddiford (9)   99
Rebekah Harvey (10)   99
Joanne Boulton (9)   100
Paige Walters (9)   100
Molly Jenkins (9)   101
Sophie Bolton (9)   101
Charlotte Anne Brankin (9)   102
Nathalie Moore (10)   102
Beth Staley (10)   103
Catherine Brankin (10)   103
Katie Gowen (11)   104
Oliver Pagington (10)   104
Ryan Mackereth (9)   104
Zoe Potts (10)   105

Novers Lane Junior School

Jessica Davey (7)   105
Luke Sheehan (9)   106
Chelsea Cox (8)   106
Lauren Travanti (9)   106
Jack Bushby (9)   107
Toni Pring (8)   107
Billy-Joe Wring (8)   107
Tatiyanna Knight (9)   108
Carla Griffin (9)   108
Melissa Smithers (8)   109

James Whittaker (9)   109
Jenny Hill (8)   109
Jiorgia Fitton (11)   110
Katie Willett (9)   110
Samantha Hunt (9)   111
Skye Lewis (8)   111
Hollie Christian (8)   111
Jordan Porter (9)   112
Tamara Eddy (9)   112
Kealy Lea (9)   113
Lauren Day (8)   114
Ben Llewellyn (8)   114
Taylor Ann Morgan (9)   115
Kayley Grist (9)   116
Roxanne Gregory (9)   116

Oldbury-On-Severn Primary School

Harvey Arnold (9)   117
Emily Jessop (11)   117
Cameron Proctor (11)   117
Joe Porter (11)   118
Daniel Bond (10)   118
Harry Collin (10)   118
Carys Harvey (9)   119
Alex Gaston (10)   119

St Anne's Park Primary School

Amy Fillingham (10)   120
Clariss Morgan (10)   120
Jessy Waller (10)   120
Yvette Rees (9)   121
Kelly Courtney (10)   121
Abigail Wren (10)   122
Chloe Johnson (11)   122
Ashley Hutchison (10)   122
Alexandra Mlewa (9)   123

Two Mile Hill Junior School

Jack Hodges (9)   123
Daniel Cotton (11)   124

Demi Heaven (10)   144
Hannah Smale (11)   145
Elsie Elder (9)   146
Sarah Giddings (11)   147
Jamie Coatsworth (9)   148

Weston Park Primary School
Gemma Challenger (10)   148
Ceri-Mai Shepherd (10)   148
Dale Hill (10)   149
Rebecca Jenkins (11)   149
Katy Weech (9)   150
Lauren Walker-Staynings (10)   150
Charlotte Reed (10)   151
Luke Jones (10)   151
Oliver Rush (10)   152
Daniel Jewell (11)   152
Joseph Stewart (11)   152
Jack Randall (10)   153
Zachary Fredericks (11)   153
Hannah Weekes (9)   154
Alex McGill (10)   154
Kara Houson (9)   155
Molly Scull (10)   155
Deakon Richards (10)   156
Jack Finney (11)   156
Sophie Wheeler (10)   157
Jamie Hawkins (10)   157
Reece Godfrey (11)   158
Amy Hart (11)   158
Ewan Estcourt (9)   159
Gemma Chandler (11)   159

The Poems

My School

My school is very good
Along with all my friends
Loads of girls and boys
Everyone is happy

Megan is very funny
And full of laughter too
So is Immy along with Mrs Pimmy
My teacher for gym is called Mrs Jimmy.

In the playground children jump and skip
And hop around all day
There's loads of happiness and laughter
Along with all the joy!

Finally I'm sad to say
It's time to say goodbye
We push all the chairs in, we all say goodbye
I'm about to cry!

Freya Hynam (8)
Bishop Road Primary School

Horses Racing

Horses racing round and round
Jumping over the big fence.
Tiny foal needs defence.
Pacing round the wide, wide paddock.
Coming up to the end.
Thank you for racing me around, my friend.

Hannah Mitson (8)
Bishop Road Primary School

Hogwarts

Hogwarts is a wizarding school,
The founders think it's good,
But all the students in it
Really think it's cool.
Albus Dumbledore is the headmaster
But Neville Longbottom is the big disaster.
Harry Potter is the famous one,
He's got two friends called Hermione and Ron!

Poppy Warren (7)
Bishop Road Primary School

Witches

Witches are different from you and me,
They stir their potion mysteriously.
Witches eat the weirdest things,
Slug soup, worm pies and bird wings.
A witch's hobby is to fly
Into the air
With a zoom and a boom . . .
And a noise of a hot air balloon!

Rebecca Tomes (8)
Bishop Road Primary School

Flowers

Flowers vanish in winter
They return in spring
Irises are purple and smell like lavender
Buttercups are yellow and smell like honey
Bluebells are blue and smell like raspberries
The petals are so soft and smooth.

Nina Kaur (7)
Bishop Road Primary School

Dad

There's a big old monster sitting fast asleep,
Come on Elizabeth, let's go and take a peep,
Its eyes are green and orange
They're as big as custard pies,
Its hands are green with warts on, oh what a guy.
Hang on a minute Timmy, he looks a little mad.
Hah! I've just realised . . .
It's our *dad!*

Georgia Hastings (9)
Bishop Road Primary School

There's No Time

There's no time to tie my laces.
There's no time to go places.
There's no time to see my teacher.
There's no time to take a picture.
There's no time to see my friend.
There's no time to drive round the bend.
B-b-b-b-because my gran's coming over.

Ella Palmer (8)
Bishop Road Primary School

Elegy

Gone, never to return again
No more jumping or pouncing
No more balls of string
Which brought laughter into my life.

The memories of him are never forgotten
I'll always miss him
For I loved him
Goodbye, Walter.

Josh Daniel (10)
Bishop Road Primary School

Owl

Owl is in a tree.
Owl is looking down at me.
It is a very old, crooked tree.
Under are brambles, very prickly.
Soon owl is off again.
He flies and flies up in the sky.
Owl is the best friend you could ever have
Because he is always there
And he is only friendly to me and *no one else.*
He spreads out his wings and screeches
Then he flies up to his nice, warm nest
At the top of our tree
In our garden.

Holly Moxham (8)
Bishop Road Primary School

Witch Hut

At the side of the old ruined castle
In the grounds
An ugly old witch can be found.
In her hut made of brick
There she can play her old known trick
On villagers who happen to pass by
She will sing her spooky old lullaby.
Next she steps out of her crooked old house
Tripping over a poor little mouse
All the villagers scream and run away
They won't be coming back another day!

Caitlin Carolan (8)
Bishop Road Primary School

The Maid

In a dusty room
At the top of the house
A maid awakens
From a wooden bed.
She makes the bed
And helps cook
And cleans the kitchen floor
Clears up the plates
And opens the door.
A woman steps in
On the sparkling floor.
High heels, tall and a long black cloak.
At teatime bread and water
All she gets
Then up to her room
And flops down on her bed.

Maya Wallis (8)
Bishop Road Primary School

A Bad Memory

I am not so fond of Easter Day
Since that's when I was told
The blood was spilt, the heart was cut
Alfie was left to mould.

My neck felt twisted
My throat was gone
My eyes were burning
My words were wrong.

No more warm fingers on a freezing day
After being licked all around
A silent kill, a horrible death
A murder with no sound.

Gabriella Inez Scott (9)
Bishop Road Primary School

Monsters!

Monsters, monsters are very scary
Monsters, monsters are sometimes hairy.
Werewolves are monsters
They come out at a full moon
Which is very, very soon.
Werewolves really like to eat big chunks of human meat.
Bogey monsters are terribly ugly
They are really not very cuddly.
Witches are sometimes green
We know 'cause they're always seen.
Witches are very, very keen
Which makes people think they're mean.
Vampires drink lots of blood
Even from their brand new bud.
Vampires can change into bats
Which are terrible to pat.

Joe Clayton (7)
Bishop Road Primary School

The Day The Cobra Came To School

The day the cobra came to school,
The girls all shrieked out sickly,
The boys just legged it quickly.
The teachers trudged out worriedly,
The cleaners ambled horridly.
The caretakers kaffufled out crazily,
The deputy ruffled out lazily.
The nursery stampeded vigorously,
The infants crashed out ridiculously.
The head yelled out loudly,
The Year 6s charged out proudly.
I just stroked it calmly,
I found out it was a toy.

Jethro Lundie-Brown (9)
Bishop Road Primary School

Midnight

A time of night
When people fight
So when it's midnight
Let the sight of the mighty fight begin.
Midnight is the best time of night
So switch on a light
At this time of night
So it doesn't give you a fright.

Joseph Pearce (7)
Bishop Road Primary School

My Cat

My cat is called Squeaky.
My cat is bouncy and cool.
My cat is scared most of the time.
My cat mostly likes to sleep.
My cat loves to eat.
My cat is asleep.
My cat is scratchy and sleek.

Ellie Daniel (8)
Bishop Road Primary School

Isobel's Rabbit

Floppy ears like cotton wool.
Eyes like the sun.
Cute humour like a newborn cub.
Greedy like a pig.
Playful as a kitten.
Hopping like a ballerina
But most of all he's all mine.

Emily Leitch (8)
Bishop Road Primary School

My Grandpa

My grandpa liked poetry,
So I half write this for him,
He was very jolly,
And to me made the sun shine in.

One night he left us,
When we saw him the next day,
On his face lay a smile,
But sadly he had passed away.

Millie Cook (10)
Bishop Road Primary School

Winter Poem

Snow settles on the ground
Hats and scarves lost and found
Frozen lakes and frozen puddles
Children run around in huddles
Cats lie on their warm rugs
Christmas trees and Christmas lights
Light the dark and gloomy nights.

Fionnuala Deasy (10)
Bishop Road Primary School

She's Gone

She lies silent, still and safe
Her cold heart cries for help
She lies hurt and sad for life
Deep down she desperately hopes
Wishing for her life back
The fun memories that she had
Going, going, gone!

Amy Nicholls (9)
Bishop Road Primary School

He's Gone

He's gone,
He's gone far, far away
I think he's gone to a better place
But I'll never see him again
Never again!

He used to live in my house
Each day I would watch him swim around
With his little friends in the tank
Sometimes I would even watch him sleep
Floating in the water
But now he's gone
I'll never see him again
Never again!

I was the one who fed him
Sometimes I would forget
But I don't think he used to mind
I really, really do miss him
The only way I can see him is when I am asleep
But when I wake up I find out that I was only dreaming
I really, really do miss him
I'll give anything to have him back
But I know he won't come back
Never again!

Emily Lo (9)
Bishop Road Primary School

Death

Cold as stone,
Still as a statue,
Crimson blood dripping
Like a tap.

Elizabeth McNamara (8)
Bishop Road Primary School

From A Railway Carriage

Flying by on the twisting road,
Watching the sad, hopeless toad,
Look at the woman rushing around,
Listen to the train's racing sound.
There is the cold, flowing river,
Cold enough to make me shiver,
And here are the people,
Walking by the steeple,
The sheep's wool flows in the air,
There is the beggar thinking life isn't fair,
There is the cat prowling along,
There is a gentleman singing a song,
The snowflakes whizz by,
There is a mother giving a sigh,
There is a man who gives a laugh,
There is a small baby calf,
There is a field of polar bears,
There are some children making dares,
There is a small bunny,
There is its cautious mummy,
The train is slowing down pretty quickly,
I try a chocolate that's a bit sickly,
Now I hear a high-pitched sound,
There is the station, it is found!

Megan Thomas (10)
Bishop Road Primary School

Lion

There was a silly lion
Who was very crazy
He sat down on his bed
For he was very lazy!

Molly Goldblatt Bond (7)
Bishop Road Primary School

The Day The Cobra Came To Assembly

The day the cobra came to assembly . . .
The vicar veered out vertically,
The cook charged out chefly.

The boys banged out badly,
The girls galloped out giddily.

The nursery nee-nawed out naughtily,
The Year 6s sixed out smugly.

The teachers tornadoed out teachingly,
The head headed out headfirstly.

The janitor jostled out jellily,
The books bounced out bookly.

The pens penned out pennly,
The mice mapped out madly.

The spiders scuttled out sideways,
The school guinea pigs left their pet pastries.

I patted the cobra on the head.
He came home with me instead.

Ellamae Lepper (8)
Bishop Road Primary School

Monday's Child

Monday's child is full of pace
Tuesday's child is full of grace

Wednesday's child will be cross
Thursday's child will always boss

Friday's child is rather clever
Saturday's child will be naughty forever

But the child that was born on the Sabbath day
Will always eat a lot of hay.

Jack Coley (9)
Bishop Road Primary School

My World

The playground is boring,
All the chains on the swings are broken.
There is a tall brick wall around the playground.

Everybody's shouting,
The wind is whistling.
The clouds are grey and steamy.

I wish there were sounds of birds tweeting,
And there were ponds with fish and ducks.
I wish there were hills and hills with butterflies and peacocks.

The sun is glittering and beaming onto the grass.
There are no clouds in the bright blue, gleaming sky.

The grass is green and lush.
I can hear grasshoppers squeaking.

In my world there are no noisy, crazy kids,
And there are no adults either.
I'm in my own world!

Isabelle Grear (9)
Bishop Road Primary School

Monday's Child

Monday's child has a big brain
Tuesday's child is a pain

Wednesday's child is a fool
Thursday's child doesn't rule

Friday's child drives a train
Saturday's child is insane

But the child that is born on the Sabbath day
Is amazing at football and a great DJ.

Fergus Robertson (8)
Bishop Road Primary School

Moving Away

A week ago I moved away,
I did not want to stay,
I phoned my friends every day,
It just never was the same.

All my friends were left behind,
'Cause I had suddenly moved on,
They still have each other,
It just never was the same.

Now the only way I can see them,
Is through plate glass in a picture,
Which lies still on my table,
Not real people either,
But I guess that will have to do.

The memories are now fading for
It will never be the same,
Because I miss them,
I wonder if they miss me too?

Ilona Butt (10)
Bishop Road Primary School

Monday's Child

Monday's child is full of pain.
Tuesday's child has a brain.

Wednesday's child is full of grace.
Thursday's child won the race.

Friday's child is full of muscles.
Saturday's child always snuffles.

But the child that was born on the Sabbath day
Shall always pay and play.

Sarah Harris (9)
Bishop Road Primary School

Bye Spike

'Spike, here boy,
Where are you?
He must be in the garden.
Spike, here boy.'

He's nowhere to be found,
I've asked everyone.
He's . . . no, he can't be,
He's dead!

'Mum, Dad, where are you?
I'm very sad, Spike's dead,
Why did this happen to me?'

My life freezes into a cold ice cube,
I'm imprisoned in fear,
It feels like time has frozen,
I lock myself in the cage of sadness.

Did it really happen to me?
If it did, I must die myself,
My life is over, I feel emotionless.

Sam Pomeroy (9)
Bishop Road Primary School

Monday's Child

Monday's child is full of pity
Tuesday's child is very pretty

Wednesday's child is very naughty
Thursday's child is very sporty

Friday's child is very cool
Saturday's child is such a fool

But the child who was born on the Sabbath day
Is extremely good at handling clay.

Sam Dickinson (8)
Bishop Road Primary School

A Day At School

Get to school.
Right on time.
Be here before 9.

Out in the playground.
Frosty wind in the air.
Nits and bits in your hair.

Teacher claps.
Line up fast.
Go as quick.
Don't be last.

Lunchtime at 12 o'clock.
Out they go in a flock.

In a happy mood.
Scoff up your food.

Clapping time.
Happens again.

Harry Mclellan (9)
Bishop Road Primary School

Dotty

Dotty doesn't live anymore
Her cage lies empty
Her bedding cold and damp.

Dotty doesn't live anymore
She is in my back garden
Under brown soil.

Dotty doesn't live anymore
She was the best hamster in the world
No one could ever replace her.

Dotty doesn't live anymore!

Emma Coode (10)
Bishop Road Primary School

Grandpa

Click - the latch on the door falls into place,
Thud - heavy footsteps stride down the hall,
Squelch - brown leather boots press mud into the carpet
        on the stairs,
Creak - I climb down the ladder and out of bed,
Squeak - the handle of my bedroom door turns,
Swish - the heavy green curtains of my window are pulled back,
Thump - Dad sits on my white painted chair,
No noise - I sit waiting for Dad to say something,
Gasp - I'm shocked at the news Dad brings,
Sob - I am sad to hear that Grandpa is dead.

Ruth Eleanor Newns (9)
Bishop Road Primary School

Dippy

Dippy was my dog, Dippy was my dog
Every day we used to play
Life was fun with little Dippy
But one day he went away and did not come back.

I wanted little Dippy, I missed him that night
It was next morning that gave me a fright
I was walking in the field when I saw a horrid sight
My poor little Dippy was lying on the floor
With not a twitching of his nose or a movement of his jaw.

Jack Hird (9)
Bishop Road Primary School

The Light Of Life

The blackness springs its trap
The dirty deed is done
For it puts out the candle of life
For her and for me.

Cameron Alsop (10)
Bishop Road Primary School

Bishop Road

B ishop Road is my school.
I like the ice cream after school.
S hops, oh I like shops.
H ope in getting all my tests right.
O h I'm so glad the day's over.
P hew! The toilets smell!

R ahh, these crisps are good.
O h no, I'm getting told off by the headmaster.
A hh, they took my ball.
D ear Lord, the ice cream van's gone!

Natasha Taylor (10)
Bishop Road Primary School

Floppy

Floppy was my rabbit, he was very cool
He messed around with wool
When it was very cool
Floppy was cool.

He watched us run around
He listened to each and every sound
And when he had his food
He ate every single round.

Floppy, he's gone and never coming back.

Aman Singh (9)
Bishop Road Primary School

Gone But Not Forgotten

Gone but not forgotten
I remember I used to buy her sweets
But now I don't get her anymore sweets
Because I can't hear her heartbeat.

Shuayb Mahood (9)
Bishop Road Primary School

Monday's Child

Monday's child is smart and clever
Tuesday's child will live forever

Wednesday's child lives under a cloud of rain
Thursday's child is a really annoying pain

Friday's child is a fast, sporty person
Saturday's child has a curse on

But the child that was born on the Sabbath day
Is rather smart, sporty and gay.

Sean Crawford (9)
Bishop Road Primary School

Monday's Child

Monday's child is big and bold,
Tuesday's child is as good as gold,

Wednesday's child ignores everything,
Thursday's child wears a rubber ring,

Friday's child is really mad,
Saturday's child is just as bad,

But the child that is born on the Sabbath day
Always seems to find a way.

Ethan Evans (9)
Bishop Road Primary School

A Limerick

There was a young boy called Bob
Who tried to steal a corn on the cob
He went into the room
He saw a broom
And was caught by a very big mob.

Alastair Monk (9)
Bishop Road Primary School

Monday's Child

Monday's child is a dude
Tuesday's child is very rude

Wednesday's child is a champion at chess
Thursday's child makes a big mess

Friday's child is very bold
Saturday's child is always cold

But the child that was born on the Sabbath day
Hates staying in and goes out to play.

Charlie Williams (9)
Bishop Road Primary School

Monday's Child

Monday's child gets detention
Tuesday's child I shouldn't mention

Wednesday's child has lots of fun
Thursday's child always knows none

Friday's child is a devil
Saturday's child isn't called Nevil

But the child that is born on the Sabbath day
Is naughty and crafty and has to pay.

Oliver Dann (9)
Bishop Road Primary School

Seasons

Spring is chilly when the lambs are born.
Summer is sunny and there is frog spawn.
Autumn gets colder and the days aren't hot.
Winter I think the snowmen are top!

Nuala Keohane (8)
Bishop Road Primary School

The Day The Cobra Came To Assembly

The day the cobra came to assembly . . .

The teachers went out teachably
The cleaners went out cleanly

The Year 6s went out successfully
The cooks went out cockily

The Year 5s went out chickingly
The Year 4s went out quickly

The Year 3s went out eating peas
The Year 2s went out from the loos

The Year 1s went out with their mums
Reception went out sucking their thumbs

But last of all the nursery went out noisily.

Joe Widdecombe (9)
Bishop Road Primary School

The Day The Cobra Came To Assembly

The day the cobra came to assembly . . .
The juniors jumped out joyfully
The mice squeaked out slowly
The cleaners climbed out clumsily
The caretakers carted out calmly
The infants hacked out harshly
The nursery tailed out tightly
The boys bounded out bravely
The head hammered out hastily
The deputy charged out cunningly
The teachers stomped out insanely
The parents waddled out wildly
I went out tiredly
The classes cried out constantly
The cobra carried on calmly.

Christopher Sainsbury (8)
Bishop Road Primary School

Who Is Under The Stairs?

I hear this creaking noise,
It's coming from under the stairs.
Who is making the noise?
It cannot be a monster or a bear.
I wondered to myself if I should go any further.
Feeling very brave I went to have a little peep.
Feeling very nervous by now
I had a little peep through the keyhole.
I saw nothing except darkness.
Wanting to go back to bed
I opened the door
And saw my friend lying in bed
Reading some books.
Feeling a little bit embarrassed
I crept up to my room.
Clank! What was that?

Megan Lockhart (8)
Bishop Road Primary School

The Evil Coat!

It was a windy day . . .
For that my coat flew away . . .
Soaring in the air,
As big as a *grizzly bear!*
It's scary and it's black,
I tried to catch it in a sack,
I saw its horrible face,
And its teeth covered with plaque.
I heard screeching in my ear,
And my mind cowered with fear.
Suddenly the wind stopped,
And the screeching coat just popped.
With its greasy head, mouldy and dead,
　　　　　I was no longer scared of bed!

Elie Ben-Shlomo (8)
Bishop Road Primary School

Monday's Child

Monday's child is very bossy.
Tuesday's child is very spotty.

Wednesday's child is very smart.
Thursday's child is good at art.

Friday's child likes chess.
Saturday's child loves tests.

But the child that was born on the Sabbath day
Is as clever as ever, OK?

Katerina Nicholson (8)
Bishop Road Primary School

Monday's Child

Monday's child is a fool,
Tuesday's child is cool.
Wednesday's child is smart,
Thursday's child likes art.
Friday's child is a pain,
Saturday's child is insane.
But the child who was born on the Sabbath day
Is so lively she hates to play.

Ella Voke (9)
Bishop Road Primary School

The Funfair

I went to the funfair on a bright, sunny day,
There were roller coasters as tall as mountains
And swing seats going as fast as speed boats,
And the best stall of all, the candyfloss stall,
Puffy clouds of bright pink candy,
I had to have some . . .
So I did!

Anna Soffe (7)
Bishop Road Primary School

Register Time

We come to school at half-past nine,
We all come in a very straight line,
It's hard for us to find a seat!

Register time is at three-quarters past nine,
Everyone wants to chat about this or that,
Mrs Pat gets annoyed,
She tells us that if you don't listen
You won't learn!

Laura Lane (8)
Bishop Road Primary School

My School Holiday

I went to hot Hungary
I went to cold Canada
I went to my gran's house
And there was a calendar.

My gran lives in France
My nan needs a chance
Because Hungary is hot
And Canada is cold
And all the rest are so, so old.

Sally Best (8)
Bishop Road Primary School

Monkey

M onkeys are smart,
O range ones are funny,
N ever stay still,
K eep away from them,
E very day they eat insects,
Y ou should like them.

Harry Magill (9)
Bishop Road Primary School

Greedy Graham

What Graham had for dinner:
6 sausages (roasted)
12 bowls of chicken legs (basted)
18 chilli pods (hot)
24 scorpion tails (the lot)
And 30 specially tempting bags of sweets

His parents, eating just one chip
Laughed a bit but very quick
Then said, most distinguishly,
'Don't eat any more, it'll kill you.'

But he still went on and on and on
He ate the universe's army
Then he went really barmy

His parents, eating just one chip
Laughed a bit but very quick
Then said, most distinguishly,
'Don't eat any more, it'll kill you.'

But he killed they say
And went all day
Drinking the Mississippi River.

His parents, eating just one chip
Laughed a bit but very quick
Then said, most distinguishly,
'Don't eat any more, it'll kill you.'

Now he really was full up
And so hid in a ditch
And died
Just eating one small chip!

Grace McNamara (8)
Bishop Road Primary School

The First Day Back At School

As the school bell chimes
Everyone rushing in on time.
Shut the windows firm and tight
Keep all your parents out of sight.

As the teacher hangs up her hat
And tells you to do this or that
Now she has told you her name
And that she will never be the same.

As you rush to your drawer
And get scissors to score
Now we're doing PSHE
We are keeping our bodies healthy.

Rush to lunch
Your orange juice in a scrunch
Next is going to the library
Then do ancient history.

Franklin Taylor Moore (9)
Bishop Road Primary School

We Lost The Game

We lost the game
It's me to blame
I thought I had so much fame
That's why we lost the game

We lost the game
Because of what's his name
Well, he's the one to blame
That's why we lost the game

We won the game
The other team lost in shame
No one to blame
We won the game.

Charlie Taylor (8)
Bishop Road Primary School

School Time

Time for school
Get up fast
Eat your breakfast
Make it last

Do your teeth
Put on your shoes
Brush your hair
No time to lose

Start to walk
Or go in the car
Whatever you do
It can't be far

Answer the register
Open your books
You're messing around
And the teacher looks

Time for play
Running around
When you come in
Don't make a sound

Time for lunch
You just can't wait
Sit up to the table
Don't be late

After lunch
It's time for play
Do some work
'Til the end of the day

And now it's home time,
That's our school day in rhyme!

Anna Murphy (9)
Bishop Road Primary School

School Time

Be on time
Here at nine
Register starts
Quick and fine
Maths and literacy
Playtime at last
Teacher's clap
Line up fast.
Down to swimming
Have a swim
Jumping out with a grin
Back to school
12 o'clock
Lunchtime lasts
Till 1 o'clock
Silent now
Register starts
Read a book
Read it fast
Teacher's saying
To the carpet
Now we're
Learning about
The Arctic
Half-past three
At last I see
My mum
She just walked past.

Annie Rolt (9)
Bishop Road Primary School

Greedy Grace

Greedy Grace loved to eat,
As a baby she ate feet,
Greedy Grace wanted more,
So she ate the kitchen door,
Greedy Grace liked to munch,
She ate bananas by the bunch,
Greedy Grace loved to eat,
She ate everything (mainly meat).

Now that she is twenty-one,
All she has left is one iced bun.

Cristina Sved-Dures (9)
Bishop Road Primary School

The Dolphin

See that dolphin loop-the-loop,
See that dolphin go poop, poop,
See that dolphin fly so high,
See that shadow in the sky,
See that dolphin swim so fast,
See that dolphin, he's coming last,
Sweet little dolphin, I have to go,
I hope you'll swim right down low.

Anna Bunting (8)
Bishop Road Primary School

Psalm To My Mum

You cheer me up when I am down
You protect me from all harm
You read to me every night
And you make me so bright
When I'm in danger your soul is always with me
I could never live without you Mum.

Guy Remmers (9)
Bishop Road Primary School

Hunter Mouse

The little mouse scampers out of his hole
He scuttles across the floorboards, heading for the fridge
Someone comes, the mouse hides behind the table's leg
The person opens the fridge
The mouse squeals and jumps and hides behind the cheese
He nibbles the cheese till it's small enough to carry
Then he takes it to his starving family.

Lara Coode (7)
Bishop Road Primary School

The Witch

As she swoops through the lamp lit sky
She cackles as she says,
'Hubble, bubble, cat's whiskers and toad's foot.'
She spies a little trick or treater.
She casts a hypnotising spell on him.
He gives a little shout before he's a frog!
She carries on through the Hallowe'en night sky.
Her kitten gives a little miaow as they glide away.

Elizabeth Vise (7)
Bishop Road Primary School

Friends

Friends are nice.
Friends are friendly.
Friends are great fun to play with.
Friends are forgiving.
Friends are great to have around to play and dinner.
I love my friends when they help me up when I've fallen down.
My friends love me too.
I love my friends, do you?

Katie Barrett Powell (7)
Bishop Road Primary School

Best Friends

When we separated classes I *really* couldn't bear
Though you looked like you didn't care
I've known you since I was one
But now look what you have done

I thought you wouldn't hide a secret from me
When you did I felt like I'd been stung by a bee
I thought I knew every story you told
But I found you had much more to hold

I told you every secret of mine
And now they're all bye-bye
I thought you were really kind
Now I think I've changed my mind

We said we would stay together
We said we would be friends forever
But now you play with other girls
You acted as if you were made of pearls
I thought you were my best friend
But now our friendship should end.

Suki Penrose Britton (9)
Bishop Road Primary School

Eating The World

There was a selfish boy
Who would like to eat a toy
He would always eat his dinner
And would never be a competition winner
He ate a terrible chocolate bar
He was on his way to eat a jar
He ate a fat fish
Even the dish
He travelled all day
And ate all the way.

Mehreen Siddique (8)
Bishop Road Primary School

The Sound Stealer

(Based on 'The Sound Collector' by Roger McGough)

A robber came this morning
Dressed in pink and red
He put every sound in a box
And left them in his shed

The shouting of my friend's dad
The bouncing of the balls
The ball against the bat
The banging on the walls

The purring of the cat
The splashing of the swimming pools
The man who grumbles because he's fat
The cool father calls

The teacher wants me to answer a fact
And that's the end of that.

Lawrence Pryn (9)
Bishop Road Primary School

The Enor-Mouse

Our class have earned a mouse,
And it's even bigger than a house!
It always drinks wine,
To make its fur *shine!*

It's very, very lazy,
When the weather's hazy!
And when we go into town,
It stomps *round and round!*

We saw it behind the computer,
Gnawing on a piece of butter,
And when I told the head,
He almost fell flat *dead!*

Luke Stafford (9)
Bishop Road Primary School

The Super Sound Stealer

(Based on 'The Sound Collector' by Roger McGough)

Without a phone call or warning
A stranger came today
He put loads of sounds into a bag
And then he went away.

The screaming of the children
The swaying of the tree
The drumming of the feet
The whooshing of the breeze.

The whipping of the skipping rope
The banging of the football
The groaning of the teacher
The crumbling of the wall.

The crunching of the leaves
The chomping of the chocolate bars
The clapping of the teacher's hands
The brooming of the cars.

Without a phone call or warning
A stranger came today
He didn't leave a sound in sight
And then he went away.

Natasha Simmons (9)
Bishop Road Primary School

The Snowman

I made a snowman very round
And fixed it securely in the ground.
But then one day the sun came out
And bashed poor snowman about.
So then the snowman was no more
Than a pile of water on the floor!

Tom Bentley (7)
Bishop Road Primary School

Rupert

A dog I had,
A lovely one
Dead he is,
Don't know where he was buried,
Put down,
Ill,
Sad,
Old,
Missed very much,
It's not the same anymore,
No more walks,
No more sticking heads out of windows,
No more riding Rupert,
No more licking faces,
17 years,
Gone forever.

Baisha Copeman (9)
Bishop Road Primary School

A Snowman

A snowman round and fat
Grumpy, gloopy, always angry
Always in my classroom, always by my side.

He never stops following me
He's with the other snowmen.
He thinks winter's cold, dusty and dirty
But it's . . .
Sparkly, cold, bright.
Winter's gone, the snowman's gone.
What am I to do?
Goodbye, winter!

Umay Habiba Zaman (8)
Bishop Road Primary School

The Cat

Climbing up trees
Chasing all the bees.
Eating fishes
In big blue dishes.
Being chased by dogs
Into big bogs.
Climbing up a fence
Ready for defence.

But most of all
Having
    A
       big
          big
             big
                cuddle
                   with
Me!

Katy Ruck (8)
Bishop Road Primary School

Chinese Festival

I'm in the street for the Chinese festival,
It's quiet,
Too quiet.

I can see something.
It's big.

It's round,
With fiery red scales.

It snakes through the courtyard
Coming closer,
And closer,
It's the Chinese dragon!

Karis Hodgson (9)
Bishop Road Primary School

Ode To Pancakes

P ancakes are perfect for tossing to the sky
A nd you have to make sure you don't toss them too high.
N ot long now until it's time to eat;
C hoose your topping - it's no mean feat!
A topping of strawberries and cream? Yes please!
K ing-sized peppers and cottage cheese?
E ach one's great but I have a dream.
S o get ready for a sugar and lemon supreme!

Georgey Stuart-Mullin (9)
Bishop Road Primary School

The Sea Serpent

The sea serpent glides underneath the crashing waves.
Slimy green scales bobbing up and down.
As blood dribbles from his gaping mouth
Fishes and sharks scarper.
The sea serpent doesn't notice the gleaming harpoon.
It sinks into his green flesh.
As the sea serpent sinks, blue blood drips!

Jan Monks (8)
Bishop Road Primary School

Ocean

Flowers and butterflies
Nettles and bees
Down beneath the ocean
Like rattles and keys
If you look closely
You'll see there's no end
To water and fishes
And the message they send.

Rosalind Barnett (9)
Bishop Road Primary School

A World Of Make-Believe

There's monsters on the stair
And goldfish on the best armchair
There's someone on my bed
And green slime on my ted
There're big brown bears
With very spiky hairs!
But wait a second
Wait a minute
Dad's turned into a big, fat *zinnet!*

Maddy Tickell (8)
Bishop Road Primary School

The Snow Is Coming

Snow is cold.
Snow is like icing on a cake.
Snow is like ice.
Snow is fun to be in.
Snow is a cold feeling.
Snow is very fun.
Snow is soft like a blanket.
Snow is soft and comfortable.

Charlotte Fry (7)
Bishop Road Primary School

Chui

Your sleek legs will soon rest.
Your tail will swish no more.
Your eyes will look at nothing.
Your tongue will taste no more.
Your ears will never hear again.
One day you will go.
But you will never be forgotten.

Isabelle Fenner (9)
Bishop Road Primary School

The Day The Cobra Came To Assembly

The day the cobra came to assembly
The boys bolted out badly
The girls skipped out sadly
The Year 2s waddled gladly
The teachers went out madly
The Year 6s stamped out swiftly
The cleaner stumbled out quickly
The head teacher rolled out proudly
The deputy head ran out soundly
The pencils pencilled out rustily
The pens penned out crustily
The monitors monitored out naughtily
The students went out haughtily
But I went and gave it a pat
While the snake man ran in like a rat.

Ansaar Malik (9)
Bishop Road Primary School

Football Crazy

Football is cool
Football is fun
You play football with a big white ball.

I like football
My friends do too
So do my family
Even my dog likes football
It's true!

I like Liverpool
My friends like Man U
My gran likes Chelsea
Do you?

Dougie Murdoch (8)
Bishop Road Primary School

The Candy Snow

On one morning I awoke,
Snow, snow, it had to be a joke!
I stood there by the window ledge,
Over there, there was a sledge!
After breakfast, in a rush,
Heard a polar bear, now hush!
Let's have a skiing fight,
Please, it isn't near to night!
Over the town the spreaders go.
Snow, snow, snow, snow, snow!
The houses look like birthday cakes,
Sprinkling sugar on the lakes!
But deep, deep, deep in the dare,
It looks like an ice cream bear.

Cara Vaitilingam (7)
Bishop Road Primary School

Rugby

Rugby, rugby, I can't be beat
Rushing by the sideline
Using my quick feet
I am very big
I can't be taken down.

It is very tense
The crowd is wild
The ball is flying up and down
I can see the try line
Wham!
Oh no, I'm a mud monster!

Gus Lloyd (9)
Bishop Road Primary School

My Grandad

My grandad is older than me
My grandad is shorter than me
My grandad is more wrinkly than me
My grandad has less hair than me
My grandad can't see as well as me
My grandad gives me money when I visit him
My grandad gives me sloppy kisses
My grandad says I love you so much
I say back, 'I love you to bits!'

Rebekah Overton (10)
Bishop Road Primary School

Animals

In the jungle the lion roars
In the sky the eagle soars
Ducks go *quack, quack* in the zoo
Whilst all the monkeys go *boo, boo, boo!*

The crocodile snaps in South Africa
The sheep on the hill go *baa, baa, baa*
The cows in the field eat all the grass
When snakes silently sneak past.

Melissa Ward (7)
Bishop Road Primary School

An Evil Teacher

She was very tall
And I was very small.
She drove people away from school
And she punched people at the pool.
It would be a stroke of luck
If this teacher was run over by a truck.
She was such a fool
And incredibly cruel.

Jim Ratcliffe (9)
Bishop Road Primary School

The Haunted Ship

On a misty morning out in the grey,
I saw a spooky ship go by out on its way.
Now I am very good at swimming, so guess what I did?
I jumped right in that water, I am only a kid.
I screamed and spluttered but I couldn't stay up.
Was I dreaming or was it just luck?
A ghostly hand got me firm
I tell you, I got one germ.
Once I was pulled onto the ship
I did a front roll and a backflip.
I stood up to thank my saver
Then I realised he'd done me no favour.
All the creatures of Hell
Had joined together to ring a bell.
I walked forward and had a crash,
A very, very big bash.
Oh, my head
I want to return into my bed.
With that I returned to home
I realised my house was in Rome.
I woke up in my bed.
It was all a dream.
Oh, but my head!

Jack Redpath (9)
Bishop Road Primary School

Juniper

No more climbing onto his saddle,
No more grooming his fur,
No more mucking out his stable,
No more entering him for shows.

No more patting his neck,
No more cleaning his shoe,
No more taking him to the field,
He's gone but not forgotten.

Evie Smithson (9)
Bishop Road Primary School

Pandora's Box

Pandora was a beautiful girl,
Whose life took an unfortunate twirl,
There was a certain box,
That was under key and lock,
Now Pandora had been created by the gods,
So she knew how to even the odds.
She stole the key from the table,
Sneaking down she found a label.

The label read *Keep Out!*
Pandora was full of no doubt.

Pandora ignored the label, she opened the doors,
And to her surprise she found millions of layers of floors,
Though in the middle was a tattered old box,
With thirty or more rusty locks,
But Pandora had the precious key,
Pandora was very vain as she thought,
Oh how good it is to be me.
Pandora put the key in the lock,
And imagine her shock,
When whizzing out came a sudden blur,
And it suddenly occurred to her,
The box was not such a good thing,
With that there was a sudden ping.
A hundred insects came clear,
Oh, the screams that you could hear,
As every ill in the world,
Out they all suddenly hurled.

Smoking, disease, death and drugs
It was as if they were whirling out of plugs.
And every ill in this very world,
Why, you can blame that pretty girl Pandora.

Florence Gregory (10)
Bishop Road Primary School

Guess What I Am

I'm round and small, sometimes big
I tell you where your family is
I come in shape
I come in size
If someone won me they'd be surprised
I tell your country
I tell your land
There is nothing quite so grand.

What am I?

Emily Stewart-Reid (8)
Bishop Road Primary School

Snow And Ice

Snow is magical
Ice is like some frozen spikes
Snow is like icing
Ice is like milk
Snow is like feathers falling from the sky
Ice is magical like snow
Ice, ice, snow, snow,
I'll always love you!

James Crawford (7)
Bishop Road Primary School

Tortoise

T errific tortoise,
O h, they are so cute,
R eally, they're great,
T hey're easy to please,
O h, a piece of lettuce,
I s all that they need,
S low and steady, keep your pace,
E very tortoise does a good deed.

Alasdair Marchant (10)
Bishop Road Primary School

The Man Of Sound

(Based on 'The Sound Collector' by Roger McGough)

A stranger came this morning,
Dressed in shorts of hay,
A stranger came this morning,
To take the sound away.
He took the pop of the popcorn,
The ring of the phone,
He even took the tromping of the trombone,
He took the tick of the clock,
He took the screech of the pen,
Then he went away,
And left us on our own.

Cherry Stewart-Czerkas (10)
Bishop Road Primary School

On Time

I always miss the bus
And then I get in a fuss
I look at the clock
And run round the block
I'm late for class
'Cause I'm playing with the grass.

My teacher says, 'Bad boy.'
Now I'm very full of joy
I can say
Bye-bye.

Rose Baker (7)
Bishop Road Primary School

Dragon

I saw a dragon flying
A man was on his back
The man said, 'Hey, hey, hey,'
The baby tried to flap.

The dragon flew through winter
The dragon flew through spring
The dragon flew through autumn
And the man started to sing.

The summer sun was blazing
Beside the dragon's side
The children on the beach all shouted
And the babies cried.

Genevieve Alsop (8)
Bishop Road Primary School

A Snowball In My Pocket

A snowball in my pocket
As I walk down the road.
A snowball in my pocket
As I walk back home.
I get inside my house
And see my little brother.
I give my snowball to him
And he throws it on the floor.

Patrick Collings (7)
Bishop Road Primary School

Gone But Not Forgotten

A beautiful treasure lost but not forgotten
Brown and silky thing lay in my hand
The name of my silky beauty is Nutmeg
A beautiful golden treasure, gone but not forgotten.

Isaac Harbord (10)
Bishop Road Primary School

Why?

Why do the planes come over at night?
What have we done to hurt them?
Every night we have to bomb them,
I don't know what they've done wrong.
Every night they come and then
Bang!
Mums and dads and children like me
Creep out screaming and crying.
Why do we have to do these hateful things?
I just don't know.
We search for loved ones who are buried under debris,
Like huge piles of hatred and darkness, holding helpless people hostage.
It scares me to think what disruption the bombs we drop cause.
We pilots can almost hear the hateful, sad screams,
Like the sirens they sound to try and save their helpless bodies.
Why does the fire burn?
Like climber plants strangling all good that is left.
Why do I have to hear the crackling fire?
Burning helpless people under huge mountains of debris.
Why do we have to suffer when we have done no wrong?
Why do they disrupt us?
But they won't get our country.
These people are too determined.
We will not win this war, they have courage.
We will have . . .
Victory!

Elizabeth Illing (11)
Cherry Garden Primary School

My Gecko

My gecko's called Kizzy
She's yellow and black
With spots on her back
Like leopard's skin
Her eyes are as sharp as a drawing pin
Her tail goes from fat to really thin
She hides in her tree
Ready to jump on her supper and tea
She hides in her yellow sand
Protecting her land
She lives in her warm cave
She will do anything, she's really brave
She runs really fast
And she will cast out her sharp claws.

George Yates (11)
Cherry Garden Primary School

Twister

Spiralling wind is coming my way,
I'm speechless, I don't know what to say.
Will I survive? Will I die?
Shall I run or just stand and sigh?
There's my house gone in the distance,
Now I have not any resistance.
I feel oh, so very weak!
It's so loud I cannot speak.
It is howling like a dog,
Sucking up every log.
Dark clouds are surrounding me,
Twister, please, just let me be.

Hannah Powell (10)
Cherry Garden Primary School

My Haunted Shed

Eek!
The windowpane screw fell out,
A silver cobweb was hanging in the light,
I was scared without a doubt.

Whoosh!
Ow! Something fell on me,
The light had gone out,
Oh no! I couldn't see.

Pitter!
The rain had started to fall,
It was flooding deep,
A tree fell down that was very tall.

Thump!
A spider was creeping along the wall,
Something came past,
It made my skin crawl.

Whiz!
My dad's bike wheels were twirling,
The brakes started to squeak,
What was that? A sound like purring?

Sizzle!
The shadow had disappeared
But still I was very scared
As out the window I peeped
When . . .
A black paw on the glass
And a face with pointed ears and sharp eyes.
It stared at me.

It was the same moment I realised
It was my cat!

Jonathan Dick (10)
Cherry Garden Primary School

Alice's Adventures In Wonderland

Down, down, down
Tumbling, turning and twisting
Then *thump!*

Gigantic and minute
Crying tears of sadness

Now complete chaos
But also a sad, long tale

Trapped in a house
Too small for her really

Next a caterpillar, old and grumpy
Smoking a hookah, long and smoky

A sneezy atmosphere
With a pig running wild

Messy and untidy
Just pure madness

White to red roses
Flamingos used as bats

The Mock Turtle
With his upsetting story

The lobster-quadrille dance
And beautiful soup, long and sad

A court case full of nonsense
Lots of unhelpful witnesses

Growing, growing, growing
A threat of execution

But saved by the sound of her sister's voice
What a weird dream! Alice thought to herself.

Holly Adams (10)
Cherry Garden Primary School

My Cat Smokey

I have a cat called Smokey,
She lounges everywhere,
If it's really cold outside,
She sits upon a chair.

She waits outside the kitchen,
To go and get her food,
She'll purr and purr quite loudly,
If she is in a good mood.

She'll growl at my other cat Blackie,
Until she goes away,
She sits beside the heating vent,
For most of the day.

She likes to lie in funny positions,
And have her belly rubbed,
But the one thing she really hates,
Is getting in the tub.

She really is the cutest thing,
That you'll ever see,
She has the greatest owner,
And of course that person's me!

Sophie Boulton (10)
Cherry Garden Primary School

My Ferrari

My Ferrari, turn the key in the ignition
My Ferrari, the fast and furious
My Ferrari, swiftly driving down the road
My Ferrari, speeding and racing
My Ferrari, shiny and red
My Ferrari, nos tanks in the boot
My Ferrari, red neons underneath
My Ferrari, 12 cylinder engine
My Ferrari, turbo engine
My Ferrari, 0-60 in 3 seconds flat.

Ben Filer (11)
Cherry Garden Primary School

Queen Of Hearts

The Queen of Hearts is strict
And will not take no for an answer
She will punish you, Alice
By saying, 'Off with your head!'
And she will take you to court
You will not get away
She feels she is in the right
But she is not!
She moves peacefully
And first talks quite calmly
Then if you disobey the Queen
She will go so red in the face
And if you say sorry
It is not enough
So if you pass the Queen
In your dream
Do not disobey the Queen of Hearts.

Alex Smith (10)
Cherry Garden Primary School

Who Are Surfers?

Surfers are kings of the waves
Surfers are bodyboarders
Surfers are brave
Surfers are wave masters
Surfers are wave grinders
Surfers are record breakers
Surfers are wave fighters.

Surfing is fun
Surfing is hard
Surfing is for pros
Surfing is like skateboarding but on water.

Harrison Guy (10)
Cherry Garden Primary School

Army Soldier

Marching to fight,
The time's never right,
I'm loading my pistol,
To wait for the signal.

The bell has just rung,
Now I must run, run, run,
My legs feel like lead,
I wish I was in bed.

I now have to kill,
Which makes me feel ill,
I should be with my boys,
Playing with their toys.

The tanks are now here,
And the noise, I feel fear,
Of who I have shot,
It must be a lot, lot, lot.

We have won the fight,
But the time wasn't right,
I feel tired and alone,
I just want to go home.

I am sad in my heart,
That I had to take part,
Because our lives are for living,
Not for fighting, no killing.

James Smith (11)
Cherry Garden Primary School

What Is Red?

Red is to me
The colour of our school jumpers
The colour of blood
The colour of my mum's favourite flower
And the colour of my mum's favourite top.

The colour red is bright
It is warm to me
It makes different colours.

Red is the sound of a loud bang
Red is the taste of red peppers
Red is the soft, like my old pillow
Red is the sound of the beginning of the war
Red is the taste of a spicy dinner
Red is the softness of a new jumper
Red is the sound of a heart breaking.

Red is my favourite colour.

Elliot Cumming (10)
Cherry Garden Primary School

My Friends Are There For Me

My friends are there for me, no matter what
I can trust them and they can trust me
They're there when I'm down, to cheer me up
To tell each other secrets, that no one else knows.

My friends are there for me, throughout the day
We may have some fall outs, but make up very quickly
We spend playtime together, laughing and having fun
Making each other happy and having a good time!

Friends we'll be forever, nothing will ever change
Different schools we're going to but in contact we will stay
If by any chance I lose them, nothing will be the same
Friends we'll be forever, nothing will ever change.

Abi Denham (11)
Cherry Garden Primary School

My Dog Buster

Buster died last November,
On the first to be exact.
He'll be in our hearts forever,
And that is a fact.

Buster was black and furry,
And was also very deaf.
His sight was very blurry,
His ashes are all we have left.

Buster was an old dog,
He was just fourteen.
He could barely even jump a log,
And he was never ever mean.

Buster sat by the fire,
To keep his body warm.
But now I know he's higher,
And safe from the big, cruel storm.

Georgia Cousins (10)
Cherry Garden Primary School

War

War is the sight of fear
War is a taste of destruction
War is a smell of poison gas
War is the sight of broken buildings
War can be heard in the battle
War can be heard from all round the world
War is a taste of smoke
War is a sight of fire
War is a taste of gunfire and powder.

Adam Ring (10)
Cherry Garden Primary School

My Cat

My cat used to scratch the sofa for attention,
My cat would climb up my ladder,
To curl up on my bed,
He would gobble down tuna,
And he wouldn't kill animals,
Like others,
His miaow would sound beautiful,
His fur was nice and soft,
He could jump over hoops,
And he would sometimes follow me to school,
He would be calm when he saw dogs,
And when he went to the vets,
He always had patience,
Waiting for food,
Sometimes he would make you laugh,
Sometimes he would make you cry,
In a happy way,
But now he has gone.

Alex Sellars (11)
Cherry Garden Primary School

Who Are Snowboarders?

Snowboarders are sliders
Snowboarders are stunt masters
Snowboarders are high jumpers
Snowboarders are snow masters
Snowboarders are pole gliders
Snowboarders are ice breakers
Snowboarders are skilful

Snowboarding is amazing
Snowboarding is fun
Snowboarding is cool
Snowboarding I've done!

Paul Nicholls (10)
Cherry Garden Primary School

Red

Red is the colour of a dazzling sunset
Red is the colour of a delicious apple
Red is the colour of blood on the tip of a sword
Red is the colour of the boiling sun
Red is the colour of juicy cherries
Red is the colour of burning fire
Red is the colour of a fire engine
Red is the colour of a beautiful rose
Red is the colour of my mum's dress
Red is the colour of my shoes
Red is the colour of my reading bag
Red is the colour of a love heart
Red is the colour of our cross
Red is the colour of lipstick
Red is the colour of the Manchester kit
Red is the colour of yummy strawberries
Red is the colour of traffic lights
Red is the colour of the red carpet
Red is the colour of a bus
Red is my favourite colour.
R-E-D.

Kane Fews (10)
Cherry Garden Primary School

The Kited Enzo

The Kited Enzo is fast!
The Kited Enzo is low!
The Kited Enzo, with fuel injection!

The Kited Enzo is furious!
The Kited Enzo is nosed!
The Kited Enzo has the need for speed!

The Kited Enzo is speakered out!
The Kited Enzo is turboed up!
The Kited Enzo is *pimped out!*

Stephen Andrews (11)
Cherry Garden Primary School

My Nanny

My nanny is lovely.
She loves me and my cousins.
She is always there for me.
She helps me when I'm sad.
She helped me when my cat died.
My nanny is crazy.
She laughs and cries at the same time.
She gives me warm cuddles.
I love my nanny's cuddles.
My nanny likes to laugh at the telly.
She finds Peter Kay very funny.
My nanny is kind.
She gave me Harry Potter.
My nanny is a good cook.
She makes me Sunday lunch.
My nanny has two daughters.
One is my mum, one is my aunty.
My nanny also has a son
Who is my uncle.
My nanny makes me laugh
When she plays with my toys.
But I love my nanny
Because she is my nanny.

Georgia Neill (10)
Cherry Garden Primary School

What Is War?

War is like a bomb falling
War is people being shot
War is smelling gas
War is joining the army
War is hearing the sound of death
War is seeing blood
War is houses falling down
War is the sound of a marching army
War is feeling worried
War is wearing gas masks
War is helping people
War is planes moving
War is like trying to escape from danger
War is the colour of red
War is feeling scared.

Harry Smith (10)
Cherry Garden Primary School

Army

The army uses stealth
To get around places.
They stay in trenches,
They use offroaders
To speed along.

The treads go round and round,
The guns fire and fire.
A thousand rounds a minute.
They use camouflage.

They hide behind sandbags.
They throw a grenade
And drink a little a day
Hey!
I think a war has started.

Connor Blanning (10)
Cherry Garden Primary School

I Wish I Had A Kind Brother!

I wish I had a kind brother to help me with my homework.
I wish I had a kind brother so he will not call me names.
I wish I had a kind brother so he will not fight.
I wish I had a kind brother so he will talk not shout.
I wish I had a kind brother then he will play with me.
I wish I had a kind brother to have fun with.
I wish I had a kind brother so he will tell the truth not lies.
I wish I had a kind brother to help me if I'm stuck.
I wish I had a kind brother to buy me some sweets.
I wish I had a kind brother so he would love me not hate me.
I wish I had a kind brother, I wish everyone had one!

Jessica Williamson (11)
Cherry Garden Primary School

My Sister Catherine

My much older sister Catherine
Is madder than Charlie Chaplin
She's a good one for jokes but she can't do a hoax
She's got blonde wavy hair
To which she gives way too much care
She's got sapphire-blue eyes
And a little weight round the thighs.

I love my sister so dearly
Anyone can see that clearly
The problem I'm facing now
Is almost too hard to think how
Soon she will be thirteen
And one year after that she will be fourteen
She'll be bringing home boys
And throwing away all her toys
My much older sister Catherine.

Lizzy Clarke (11)
Colston's Girls' School

Guess Who?

This person is a roaring lion,
But can be as quiet as a cloud,
This person has a sense of humour,
When he laughs out loud.

Guess who?

This person is only six years old,
Yet acts as if he's twenty-two,
This person helps himself to food,
When Mother tells him not to.

Guess who?

This person doesn't know what tidy means,
But he knows the meaning of messy,
For when he's told to tidy his room,
He starts to get all pesky.

Guess who?

This person is a relative of mine,
This person loves me madly,
This person is my younger brother,
This person is called Bradley.

Terri-Ann Bourton (10)
Colston's Girls' School

Katy's There

Katy's there,
Swinging on her chair.
Where? Where?
Over there with her long, blonde hair.

Sway, sway,
Back and forth,
Crash and bash,
She's on the floor!

Daisy Scott (10)
Colston's Girls' School

The Ghost Carriage

Riding through the dead of night
The air is filled with horrid fright
Too fast, too fast but still they go
They'll never halt or ever slow
Through the trees so filled with fog
Over the hills they head for the bog
Inside the carriage sits a bride
Her groom he sits just by her side
They start to scream
They're going to die
They're going to die
Oh, why did they do this?
Why oh why?
Then in they plunge, they'll never come out
But then we hear when they scream and when they shout for -
In the dead of the night when there is no light
When the air is filled with horrid fright . . .
They'll ride again and relive the pain
And it's always going to be the same
Riding in the ghost carriage.

Elske Waite (11)
Colston's Girls' School

Ellie Carter

Ellie Carter is my best friend:
Tall, shy, pleasant,
Like a silken cushion,
Like a pure white dove,
She makes me feel happy,
Like a bouncy red balloon.
Ellie Carter:
Some people are just perfect.

Cara George (11)
Colston's Girls' School

New School

I'm standing outside the giant gates
Which guard the giant school
I put one foot inside the grounds
And watch the massive crowds
Then I realised I'm alone
No friends, no family, no dog or phone
And there I see before my eyes
A group of strangers pass me by.

I stepped inside the classroom doors
All bright and colourful, red and blue walls
A group of kind faces greeted me
Someone offered me a sweet
Then the teacher spoke
And made a joke
No longer alone
I'm with friendly folk.

Emily Morgan (10)
Colston's Girls' School

Recycling

I am telling you to recycle
Just a simple jar
It may just be small
It could be a window of a car.

I am telling you to recycle
Just a simple can
It may just be small
It could be a van.

Isn't it incredible what recycled things can be?
So take an obvious hint
And recycle
Just like me.

Nicole Hutson (11)
Colston's Girls' School

Traffic Jam!

We're in the car and I can't wait to get home
As me and my friend want to talk on the phone!

We're going fast but then I see
Lots of red lights, what could it be?

Horns, shouting, what's in the road?
Is it a lamb?
No, I'm in the middle of a
Traffic jam!

We're slowly moving,
Now we're not at all,
Oh no, now I won't be able to make my call.

The lights are changing yellow to green
Go, go, go, I have to speak to my friend Dean.

Yes, at last
We've definitely passed
Oh no, there's another one
. . . and blast!

Rebecca Bailey (10)
Colston's Girls' School

That Piece Of Paper!

See that piece of paper
There on the floor,
Crumpled, stamped on,
Standing so small.
I wish I could use it
And make it worthwhile,
If I could it would make me smile.
I would make it colourful, bouncy
And powerful.
I would create
Something to celebrate.

Lottie Kemp (11)
Colston's Girls' School

Stay Off Building Sites

SOBS
Never play on building sites
Don't be like Tom and Mick
You might end up in hospital
Or at the local nick!

Building sites are dangerous
With lorries everywhere
The driver might not stop in time
If he doesn't know you're there.

Building sites are full of holes
There are lots of them about
And if you fall down into one
It's hard to get back out!

Diggers dig and tippers tip
While Tom and Mick just play
They'll end up in a right old mess
If they get in the way!

So please don't learn the hard way
With fractures, falls and fright
Just find a safer place to play!
But stay off building sites.

Jessica Ann Hudson (10)
Colston's Girls' School

Around The World!

(In memory of the tsunami '04)

England!
Damp and wet,
Dark and gloomy,
With never a sunset.

America!
Famous and hot,
Home of Walt Disney,
With the gossip of pop.

Mexico!
Cactus and chilli,
Sombreros and señors,
And the frocks are all frilly.

Italy!
Pizza and spaghetti,
Green, white and red flag,
And excellent espresso coffee.

Thailand!
One of the countries,
Hit by a wave,
And now they are buried in a grave.

Be grateful!
Be thankful for your country,
There are others that aren't as lucky,
So be grateful for your country,
And think of those who aren't as lucky.

Hollie Farrow (11)
Colston's Girls' School

Teachers

She has eyes like a hawk, watching for any grammatical errors.
If you spell something with an 'i' instead of an 'e',
She'll pounce like a cat.
She stalks around the class, looking over shoulders until . . .
Ring, ring
The bell goes and she leaps to her desk,
Gives out the homework and stomps out of the class,
Leaving the classroom in silence.
If she says something she's always right,
Even if she isn't quite.
She's like an owl with her glasses
Perched on the end of her nose.
I'm glad I'm taught by her,
There's no one I'd prefer.

Katie Smith (10)
Colston's Girls' School

The World Is Coming To An End

The world is coming to an end.
My mum thinks I've gone round the bend.
My dad thinks that I must be looney.
But this is not all cartooney.
Our neighbour's house has fallen down.
A lightning bolt has hit the ground.
No one will co-operate.
Oh look, there goes the garden gate!

No one understands but me.
But the world has ended - *you'll see!*

Savannah Sevenzo (11)
Colston's Girls' School

Poems Don't Have To Rhyme

Poems don't have to rhyme
You know this isn't going to rhyme
Just think of a rhythm and go with the flow
Poems don't have to rhyme.

This is a poem but not a rhyme
All you can do is think and write
This is make-believe you see
This is a poem but not a rhyme.

Listen
Poems don't have to rhyme
You can just make up a rhythm
And go with the flow.

This is only a poem
Don't get annoyed
Be calm, breathe, don't panic
After all it is just a poem!

Laura Green (11)
Colston's Girls' School

The Gran For All Seasons

I call her my gran for all seasons,
For she's like the budding blossoms of spring,
Always fresh with new ideas;

Like a breezy summer garden,
Full of colours undiscovered.

Aged and experienced,
She's like the falling autumn leaves;

My warm and cosy armchair,
On a cold winter night:

Who else but my gran . . .
For all seasons.

Khushboo Chandiramani (11)
Colston's Girls' School

Snow!

Waking one morning from my sleep,
I pulled back the curtain to take a peep.
A huge, white blanket covered the ground,
Snow was falling all around.
Leaving the warmth of my nice, cosy bed,
Down to the kitchen I hastily sped.
I was in such a hurry for I had a plan,
I was going to build an enormous snowman.
Breakfast was ready, the table was laid,
I ran to the shed for the garden spade.
I piled the snow as high as I could,
I wanted this snowman to look really good.
When I had finished I felt quite proud,
'That's a wonderful snowman,' I said out loud.
Next morning I woke and, rushing outside,
A big pool of water is what I spied.
My snowman had vanished and to my dismay,
The sunshine had melted him all away!

Katie Ahmadi (11)
Colston's Girls' School

The Mary Rose

The Mary Rose
Is a huge ship
That once sailed across the sea.
It's big and brown and ancient.
It's like a whale swimming in the sea.
It's as pretty as a butterfly
But it makes me feel small.
The Mary Rose makes us
Think of the past
And remember how lucky we are.

Becky Holt (11)
Colston's Girls' School

My Magic Box

(Based on 'Magic Box' by Kit Wright)

I will put in my box . . .
A pure gold pen,
An old oak tree racing to the sky.

I will put in my box . . .
The love of my mum,
The safety of my family,
The happiness of everybody.

I will put in my box . . .
A palm tree in Antarctica,
A polar bear in Africa.

My box is fashioned
From soft, deep velvet
With ivory hinges.

I shall hide in my box
Away from all evil
And show the world how to have peace.

I love my box!
It is so amazing,
I never want to close the lid.
I know my box will always be there for me.

Bridget McManamon (10)
Colston's Girls' School

Big Ben

Big Ben
Is a huge clock, a landmark.
It is big, loud and tall
Like a giant's finger pointing to the sky,
Loud as a tiger's roar:
Makes me feel really tiny, insignificant.
Big Ben
Makes us realise how important time is.

Francesca Seaman (10)
Colston's Girls' School

My Angel Mum

My angel mum:
She's as pretty as the word pretty,
Welcoming, loving, smiling,
Like Mother Nature,
Like a garden full of flowers.
She makes me feel special:
I'm the most important person in her world.
My angel mum
Covers me with protective wings.

Katie Johnson (11)
Colston's Girls' School

My Lion

My little white lion
Has a long tail,
Long, snowy, swishing,
Like a snake going by,
Like a wave in the sea.
I feel so warm when I'm near her,
Like the warmth of a fire.
My little white lion
Reminds me of how sweet life is.

Morag Haddow (11)
Colston's Girls' School

My Sister

My sister is a silk dress,
A pink, spotty hairclip,
A solid silver pen.
My sister: a blade of soft green grass,
A beautiful tree that is blossoming.
My sister is my friend:
I know she'll always be there for me.

Joanna Goldsack (10)
Colston's Girls' School

The Moon

The moon
Floating in the solar system,
Round, bright, shiny,
Like a bright hole leading from a dark cave
Makes me feel like a tiny star,
Makes me feel I want to jump right over it.
The moon
Makes me think someone has thrown a big ball
Way up high in the sky.

Isobel Pearce (10)
Colston's Girls' School

My Mum

She is a bird singing in a tree,
She's a pin - solid gold,
A lovely dolphin dancing on the horizon,
A hot rainforest with animals around her,
A roaring lioness looking after her cubs,
A purring kitten cuddled up.
She is a starry night.
A white horse with wings.
She will always be my mum.

Ocean Murphy (10)
Colston's Girls' School

My Rainbow

Red like the fiery opening to a vortex
Orange like the sun on a summer's day
Yellow like the sand on a lovely beach
Green like grass in the park at spring
Blue like the sky on a beautiful day
And purple, purple just makes a rainbow . . . well, a rainbow!

Ellie Smart (10)
Colston's Girls' School

A Busy Street

In the dark,
People pushing, people rushing,
Screaming children,
Babies sound asleep,
People whispering.

In the dark,
Dogs barking,
Bugs crawling around,
Dogs chasing cats and tripping people up.

In the dark,
Moon's glowing,
Wind howling,
Stars bright,
Street lights beaming.

In the dark,
Phones ringing constantly,
Cash tills dinging,
Shops about to close,
Alarms buzzing,
Have a super Christmas!

Francesca Dark (9)
Colston's Lower School

My Hamster

My hamster is a cute little chum,
His golden fur shines in the sun.
He never ever runs away,
He's always there, ready to play.

My hamster thinks he's funny,
He rolls around like a bunny,
And jumps around like a puppy,
He tries to be scary but I think he's funny.

Joshua Cox (9)
Colston's Lower School

A View From My Window

A view from my window,
There's creepy things out there,
Something's moved,
Was it a mole?
Was it my dog?
Someone just screamed,
What happened?

A view from my window,
My mum says don't go out at night,
I wonder where my dog is now,
I hope she is safe,
This is scary,
What's that noise?
Dad,
Mum,
I'm scared.

A view from my window,
I'm going to put my light on,
It's dark out there now,
It looks scary out there,
What was that just now?
It's a bat,
I hate bats.

Anna Thomas (8)
Colston's Lower School

Tornado

T errible things are in it,
O bviously it's bad,
R ipping houses, destroying herds,
N imbly it attacks,
A mbushing is good,
D estroying is everything,
O h, the trouble tornadoes cause.

Joseph Newton (7)
Colston's Lower School

The Siberian Tiger

The Siberian tiger is a fearsome cat
It sleeps in a den
Not on a blue mat
It pounces on animals
Not always mammals
Its cubs are jumpy
Playful and lively
After it catches its prey
Other animals snatch it away
It growls and fights to get it back
But doesn't always succeed against the pack
The Siberian tiger is a fascinating animal
Surviving the cold, snowy day
A shame it has to go away.

Alice Harding (9)
Colston's Lower School

My Garden At Night

Midnight looming,
Full moon crimson,
Trees rustling,
Cats miaowing
Dogs barking,
Fireworks banging,
Church bells ringing;
Gates screeching,
Teenagers scheming,
Cars racing,
Soothing stars,
Zooming cars,
Alarms waking people up,
Dawn looming.

Ben Helps (9)
Colston's Lower School

A Deserted House

Outside is dark and full of bats flying,
People screaming and spiders crawling,
Doors banging, pictures swinging,
Grass swishing and cats screaming,
Ghosts laughing,
Spiders spinning.

Outside is dark with shapes moving,
Owls screeching and creatures passing,
Creatures watching in the dark,
Bats' eyes looking for work,
Animals stealing,
Bats brooding in the trees.

Outside is dark with people screaming,
Voices calling, creatures crawling,
People dreaming in their sleep,
Sounds of people's voices,
Time is getting on,
Dawn is approaching.

Matthew Lewis (9)
Colston's Lower School

The Street

People pushing
People rushing
Families running as fast as ever
Parents are sick of looking at street lights

Children screaming
Babies asleep as quiet as ever
Mums annoyed
Horns beeping because mums are angry

Buses are busy as never before
Dogs barking and cats are scared
Street lights gleaming and phones are ringing
Cash tills never stopping for a rest.

Amanda Giles (8)
Colston's Lower School

Ferrari Enzo

The Ferrari is very fast
Looks nice from far away
It's a very cool car and looks flashy
And it's been painted blood-red
Gleams and sparkles from being truly clean
It drives far
And is very good fun
As it shines with the sun
Oops! It crashed!
Someone is saying, 'Bye-bye, Ferrari,
You were very good fun
While I had you.'

Harry Ball (8)
Colston's Lower School

Merlin

M ystery, how does he do it?
E very day he casts incredible magic spells,
R eally he's just like us,
L ater he gets his wand out and he goes, 'Caboom!'
I nteresting idea, placing an object on a rock,
N obody but Arthur could pull out the sword.

Matthew Davies (8)
Colston's Lower School

School

S chool I hate,
C ool it ain't.
H ate school as much as you can,
O h, and the lessons, man!
O h, but playtime is great,
L ike school as much as you can, mate!

Leon Worthington (8)
Colston's Lower School

The Tiger

The tiger is a fearsome cat,
He wears no shoes, nor scarf, nor hat.
The tiger pounces on 'his' prey,
Until they have all gone away.
He only lets 'his' family eat,
No one else is allowed 'his' treat.

The cubs play all day,
Never ever run away.
They never hunt for prey,
Until, they are old enough, to move away!

Jack Digby (9)
Colston's Lower School

Pancakes

P ancakes are just so great,
A nice pancake is a mate,
N ever refuse a nice pancake,
C *ome on, come one, come on, eat!*
A nice pancake is the thing to eat,
K nock on the door and you might get some more,
E very day you should eat eight,
S o, everybody, eat pancakes!

Harry Pincott (8)
Colston's Lower School

My First Day At School

My first day at school was great,
I made a friend called Kate,
We went out to play,
It was a beautiful day,
She made me laugh; she made me smile,
I think I'll stay at this school for a while!

Charlotte Attwood (7)
Colston's Lower School

The River

The river is flowing, boats sinking,
Logs floating in the dark,
Only water moving.
Stars flashing,
Waterfalls pounding,
Everything being washed away.
Leaves fall in their thousands,
Boulders sinking,
Things sinking.

The river is flowing,
Trees falling,
Fish struggling,
Twigs hitting one another,
Water rising,
Darkness closing in.

James Robinson (8)
Colston's Lower School

A Busy Street

Parents shouting,
Children stamping,
Children screaming,
Phones ringing,
Shops closing.

Cats fighting,
Dogs barking,
Horns beeping,
Cash tills dinging,
Alarms buzzing.

Cars racing,
People pushing,
Lights glowing,
People rushing,
Friends whispering.

Lily Allen (9)
Colston's Lower School

My Dog Riley

Hello, my dog
Is called Riley
He's black and
Likes to listen
To Kylie.

My dog's breed
Is a Staffie
He comes home
And shoots off to the café.

When he goes
To the park
And plays on
The swing
People look at him as
If he is a monkey king.

Cyrus Caven (10)
Colston's Lower School

Mysterious Blue

Blue is the sky at night
Stretching for miles and miles.
The moon is blue
On a foggy, dark night.
Blue is mysterious galaxies
But can also be a sunny blue sky.
Blue is a deep, dark sea
Miles of vast, open water.
Coldness is blue as
Relaxation is blue.
Blue is mysterious.
Moody.
Nothingness.

Sam Crew (11)
Colston's Lower School

Red

Red is the flesh of a ripe strawberry
And a cherry, freshly bitten.
Red is the blood that a war will spill
And a poppy waving for remembrance.
Red is the colour of an Aldington tie
And tomato soup on a cold winter's eve.
Red is a parrot in the Amazon forest
And a crab scuttling across the seabed.
Red is a ladybird flying through a garden
And an Admiral butterfly fluttering aimlessly.
Red is an apple shining in the afternoon light
And an autumn leaf blowing in the wind.
Red is the sun glowing like a house on fire
And a rose on a summer morning.
Red is a fire burning through the night
And a sunburn, glowing like a dying fire.
Red is a colour of sorrow and woe
But also a colour of joy.

Amy-Ruth Spreadbury (11)
Colston's Lower School

My Cat

My cat's life is so strange
She knows we won't cause her harm
But because she is skittish
She may bite you on the palm.

My cat's life is so strange
She runs up and down the stairs
For a bit of fun
And just misses my mum's Rupert Bears.

My cat's life is so strange
She gets chased by my rabbit
Then runs straight inside
And thinks, *that's it, I've had it!*

Jonathan Lowrie (11)
Colston's Lower School

A Piece Of Green Putty I Found In My Armpit One Morning

(Based on 'The Hitchhiker's Guide To the Galaxy')

I woke one morning,
I went downstairs yawning,
And as I sat to eat my butty,
Out from my armpit fell a piece of green putty.

It was green and slimy,
Dirty and grimy,
Squidgy and mucky
And all over my bacon butty.

So when you get up one morning,
And head downstairs yawning,
Make sure no green putty,
Falls on your bacon butty.

Philip Roy Box (11)
Colston's Lower School

Not Another Drive In The Car

When we go driving in my mother's car,
Which is nothing like a Jaguar,
We race around from place to place,
Travelling at a horrendous pace.
We arrive at school just on time,
I hope on route we didn't pick up a fine.
My legs are like jelly, I can hardly walk,
And nothing comes out when I try to talk.
I cannot move, I cannot speak,
In fact, all I feel is totally weak.
I cannot work, I cannot play,
I'm just dreading the bell at the end of the day.
Oh no, oh dear, the homeward journey is about to begin,
I'm sure if it were a race we would definitely win!

Jessica Derrick (10)
Colston's Lower School

Red

Red is anger, boiling in a pot,
Red is lava, very, very hot.

Red is blood on the vampire's fangs,
Red is alarm, for midnight bangs.

Red is a strawberry, my favourite fruit,
Red is evil, for a pursuit.

Red is a poppy, a remembrance flower,
Where relatives mourn for hour upon hour.

Red is the colour of whiteboard pens,
Red is the colour of heads on hens.

Red is the colour of a cherry,
The favourite fruit of my friend Kerry.

Red is a sunset in the sky,
Red is cherry and tomato pie.

Emma Fredericks (11)
Colston's Lower School

Puppy

Getting out of bed
Shining in the sun
I wonder where he is next
I think he's in the garden
Running in the sun
He comes indoors
To have a drink
Then he's lying by the fire
I switch off the lights
I see a pair of orange eyes
Glowing in the dark.

Joshua Wanklyn (8)
Colston's Lower School

Parrots

In a lovely
Shiny cage you find
A parrot.

Parrots are kept in
Cages and
Taught to talk.

I saw a cage one day
And what did I see?
What did I see?
A little parrot sitting on a little tree.

He tried to talk
To me
And I tried to talk
To him but
He could not hear me.

I told him to fly
And go free
And have a wild
Life!

Callum Braley (10)
Colston's Lower School

Milo

Milo
He is cute and soft.
He is as fast as a cheetah.
He runs and runs
From place to place
Never stopping unless there's food.
He's like a fish, always swimming.
After we've been on holiday
He goes mad.
He runs about and slides.

Alex Wakley (10)
Colston's Lower School

Gerbils

Gerbils, gerbils, small and sweet
Look cute when they eat.
Digging tunnels fast and fun
Keep on going till their work is done.
They nibble and gnaw like a saw
On and on even more.
They're desert rats, look like little wingless bats.

Alex Knight (9)
Colston's Lower School

Teachers

Are teachers really human?
Because I think they're walking monsters.

I don't think they know a lot,
If they did,
They wouldn't ask us how to spell,
Or ask us simple questions.

Did they really ever go to school?

Nathan Rennolds (7)
Colston's Lower School

Snakes

A snake's life is
Only worth
Half in captivity, it
Could be
A full life
If it were free.

Jemma Kinsey (10)
Colston's Lower School

The Prince

There once was a prince,
Who liked to eat mince,
Who once wanted to prance,
At a very big dance,
And has never been seen eating mince since.

Calvin Peters (10)
Colston's Lower School

At The Zoo

At the zoo the monkey looks at me
He is so cheeky, so happy.

Is it because he's got friends,
Or because he's well fed?

I will never know.

Kirby Malone (10)
Colston's Lower School

Limerick

There was once a prince quite by chance
Who thought he was good at a dance.
He said with a flounce,
'Just look at my bounce,'
And all they could see was a prance.

Cameron Nichols (9)
Colston's Lower School

Gorillas In Captivity

A black figure helpless in a cage
Its black, bushy fur suits its name
The pitch-black eyes don't move until
The moment you leave.

Just sitting there munching on lettuce or carrots
Minding their own, dawdling, whatever
The weather.

Gorillas are dark black and walk
On their hands
We are a type of them, believe it or
Not!

Just imagine what they are thinking:
'They're free, I'm stuck here!
They're watching me eat and swing on
A rope. How boring!'

Jack Pitt (10)
Colston's Lower School

Why I Hate School!

I don't like school,
So what!
The teachers are so cruel.

Why should we go to school?
It seems so stupid to us,
We even have to get up early for the school bus.

If I'm late,
Laughter comes from my mate.
If I chew gum in class,
The teacher makes me spit it out.

I'll chew some in class tomorrow,
No doubt!

David Roberts (8)
Colston's Lower School

My Hamsters

My hamster was called Merlin
He passed away on New Year's Day.

He broke one leg
By a mighty fall
It was my brother's fault.

Merlin did the monkey bars
So he was pretty fit and he had all the kit.

My hamster now is called Gary
He is a show-off
Always in his wheel.

Gary is a show-off
And never stops
In his wheel.

Merlin was the past
Gary is the present
Who knows what is to come?

In the future I may end up with another one.

Adam Henry Rivers (10)
Colston's Lower School

My Dog

I have a dog and her name is Rosie,
She is so warm and cosy
Soft and fluffy, I'm glad we had her as a puppy
She eats lots of socks
And watches all the clocks.

Rosie eats lots of food
She is so cool, she is a dude
She acts so cute
And even eats fruit
The softest things are her ears
And I'm glad that dogs live for many years.

Jessica Silman (10)
Holymead Junior School

Now The Day Is Over

Now the day is over
Night is drawing nigh
Shadows of the evening
Steal across the sky

Now the darkness gathers
Stars begin to peep
Birds and beasts and flowers
Soon will be asleep

Calm and sweet repose
With the tenderest blessing
May our eyelids close

When the morning wakens
Then may I arise
Pure and fresh and sinless
In the holy eyes.

Abbie Rose Cliff (10)
Holymead Junior School

When I Raided The Fridge

When I raided the fridge I found . . .

Apples, milk and chocolate bars,
Eggs and grapes and strawberry jam jars,
Orange juice and mouldy cheese,
Kiwi fruit and runner beans.

Margarine and Tommy K,
Tuna bake from yesterday.
Chocolate milk and mayonnaise,
Cucumber salad for sunny days.

When I raided the fridge!

Laura Perry (10)
Holymead Junior School

My Garden

In my garden,
As the howling wind blows, the rusty leaves fall,
Lying against the trees so tall.

In my garden,
The soft and gentle wind chime plays its joyful song
And dances on the friendly, thin air.

In my garden,
As the squeaky shed door opens and closes
All goes quiet and dawn becomes night.

In my garden,
The never-ending, bright green grass
Crashes against the giant feet
Of all the peaceful people walking by.

In my garden,
A lovely day goes by
And all of my spectacular garden says, 'Goodnight.'

Sabina Porter (10)
Holymead Junior School

My Mum, Your Mum

Me: 'My mum's thinner than your mum!'
You: 'But yours is bigger than mine!'
Me: 'Well, I have to agree she's as tall as a tree
        When yours is as small as a pine!'
You: Well, my mum's better at cooking!'
Me: 'I guess you got that right;
        My mum burnt her nose
        And broke four of her toes
        While making dad's cherry delight!'

Graciela Berrios- Silva (11)
Holymead Junior School

The Demon Dinner Ladies

Thump! Thump! Here comes the stampede
Of hungry children wanting a feed.
But what is this? We seemed to have forgotten our sandwiches.
We'll have to put up with the dinner lady witches!

What's on the menu
In vomitarium venue?
Eyeballs on toast,
And suspicious-looking sausage roast!

For dessert, liquorice surprise,
The surprise being it's a slug in disguise!
'What's this? We're served gristle!'
But luckily there goes the whistle!

Dinner ladies say, 'Oi, you lot, over 'ere!
We want to force into you some fear!'
We start to protest, 'Why must it be us?'
Dinner ladies reply, 'Oh, don't make such a fuss!'

Dinner ladies continue, 'Stack those chairs!'
But we reply, 'Oh, who cares?
Quickly, let's run back to class,
This whole thing has been a farce!'

Jack Chianese (11)
Holymead Junior School

Untitled

(Inspired by Frank Huntley - my grandad)

Temptation says the tide is out
But you will get across
Without a doubt
But he who treads the path of sin
Will learn how quick the tide comes in.

Jordan Cross (10)
Holymead Junior School

My Sister

My sister, what a pain! So bossy, so vain.
Always wants to have her way, never listens to a word I say.

> She is naughty,
> She is good,
> Wouldn't change her if I could.

My sister, what a noise! Always clanging on her toys.
Never wants to give and share, wouldn't care if I wasn't there.

> She is naughty,
> She is good,
> Wouldn't change her if I could.

My sister zooms around, her feet never really touch the ground.
Always running around the room, like I said, zoom, zoom, *zoom!*

> She is naughty,
> She is good,
> Wouldn't change her if I could.

My sister, into everything, a book, a shoe, a doll, a ring.
Never leaves anything alone,
My Lego, my pens, a lamp, a phone.

> She is naughty,
> She is good,
> Wouldn't change her if I could.

My sister, like no other, I am glad that I'm her brother.
She may be a rotten little brat,
But I love her and that is that.

Alex Buss (11)
Holymead Junior School

Seasons

S ee the seasons changing bit by bit
E ase the terrible coldness of winter
A utumn, summer, spring, winter,
    all have nothing in common at all
S weet and fresh is the blossoming smell of spring
O ctober is in the season of mellowing autumn
N ovember is in-between mellowing autumn and bleak winter
S easons are all different in every way.

Grace Gibbs (11)
Holymead Junior School

Old Oakey

All those years when it got hot
The kids used to sit in a nice, shady spot
Under those branches all covered in leaves
The kids used to sit and listen to the buzz of the bees
They could sit and chat on a laid out mat
Or make a fuss of the caretaker's cat
Old Oakey has now gotta go and everyone was shouting,
'No! No! No!'

Emma Francis (10)
Holymead Junior School

Miss Dowd

A mouse in the night woke Miss Dowd,
She was frightened and screamed very loud
Then she thought, *at the least*
I shall scare off the beast
And she sat up in bed and miaowed!

Amie Collett (11)
Holymead Junior School

Evacuated

The railway carriage retreating into the distance
The engine noise through the rain gives way to silence
The lines of children in unnatural stillness
Silent and motionless as a photograph
I dare to let my eyes wander
Up and down the lines of solemn and unblinking faces
My eyes prick hot
I grasp my battered and scratched suitcase
The handle slips in my sweaty hands
The lady with the hat reads the names list
And the children peel away from the group
Somebody has turned the sound off in my head
All I can hear is the pat, pat, pat, pat of my heart
In slow motion my friends leave me to my doom
'Luke Adison,' I see her mouth my name
The throat tightens, I cannot answer
'Is that you, boy?'
I nod
'Well, look lively, you're a lucky boy.'
I hate it
Give me Hitler and the Blitz
And everything I love.

Luke Addison (10)
Holymead Junior School

Sea

Splash! as the sea trembles,
The *whoosh!* of a nearby seagull,
Boom! as the sea crashes off the port,
Down goes the boat as the sea swallows,
The fish jumping and going down without a trace,
The only thing to find them,
Their destiny awaits.

James Nichol (11)
Holymead Junior School

The Zoo

When you go to the zoo
There are some things you must not do
You must not pull faces or look sad
Because it will make the monkeys mad

You must not be heard
Because it will upset the birds
You must not eat cakes
Because it's torturing the snakes

When you visit the zoo
There are some things you must do
You must make a nice wish
And it will come true for the fish

You must wear hats
Because it's respectful for the bats
You must have a good laugh
Because it cheers up the giraffes.

That's what you should do at the zoo.

Faith Evans (10)
Holymead Junior School

Flowers

Some are yellow, some are red,
On the window sill and on the cover of my bed,
Summer, winter, rain or shine,
They always seem to be absolutely fine,
Tulips, daises and roses,
Daffodils, crocus and even posies . . .

Flowers!

Samantha Mogg (11)
Holymead Junior School

There Was A Young Girl Called Joice

There was a young girl
Who wouldn't stop dancing
She'd twirl and twirl
And spend all day prancing

One early, bright morning
Joice lost her prance
She decided to sing
Not to prance or dance

One day Joice lost her voice
She could not dance or sing
What a sad girl was Joice
She said she couldn't do a thing

One day Joice woke up
And wouldn't stop dancing
She twirled on a cup
And spent all day prancing

There was a young girl
Who wouldn't stop dancing
She'd twirl and twirl
And spend all day prancing.

Taylor Bragg (11)
Holymead Junior School

Cherries

Fruity, juicy, red and green,
Tasty, sweet and make you dream,
Red as roses, green as grass,
Sharp but sweet, they always last,
Lots of lovely, fruity berries,
We all, we all, we all love cherries!

Laura Wood (10)
Holymead Junior School

The Ginger Cat

The ginger cat creeps silently closer,
Slowly through the evening shadow,
Sneaking up shyly she disappears from view,
Oh, she's jumped up to the window.

Now, much to my surprise,
She's prowling around my feet,
Her eyes sharpen, her ears rise,
Sniffing the air for a treat.

But now her mood is changing,
She purrs like never before,
No longer Miss Independent!
Now she loves me more.

She strolls right up to me,
With her head held high,
She's mooching for her tea,
She's no longer shy.

Now that she's been fed,
She seeks somewhere to lie,
She curls up silently on my bed,
Oh, she's definitely not shy!

Gabriella Aimee Cotton (11)
Holymead Junior School

The Big Squeeze

There once was a lady called Rose
Who had a big spot on her nose,
She was told not to touch
With her fingers that much,
So she squeezed it with two of her toes.

Maddie Austin (10)
Holymead Junior School

Ice Cream

Ice cream, ice cream, everyone loves ice cream
You lick it and you slurp it
And you scoff it and you burp it
Ice cream, ice cream, everyone loves ice cream

Chocolate, chocolate, everyone loves chocolate
You suck it and you munch it
And you melt it and you crunch it
Chocolate, chocolate, everyone loves chocolate

Toffee, toffee, everyone loves toffee
You chomp it and you nibble it
And sometimes you even dribble it
Toffee, toffee, everyone loves toffee.

Sprouts, sprouts, no one likes sprouts!
So I won't go on about them.

Alex Kelly (11)
Holymead Junior School

My Little Monster Cat!

She's a sneaky, black and white kitten.
Her claws are as sharp as needles.
She's a baby to Mum, a monster to me
And when we're alone she attacks me like a lion
And when my friends sleep she jumps on their face.
I think she's an alien from outer space.
My mum thinks she's a cute, fluffy kitten
But I love her!

Jade Lewin (11)
Holymead Junior School

Hope

Africa's starving,
Countries at war,
People homeless,
Millions of people poor.

But they have hope,
They strive to cope,
So when you're scared and sad,
Feelin' life is a-treatin' you bad,
When you need help to understand,
Never forget, hope will take you by the hand.

So help hope to travel this world,
Let hope expand,
Let hope help more people understand,
Take more people by the hand,
Guide them through the struggle that is life.

So when you're scared and sad,
Feelin' life is a-treatin' you bad,
When you need help to understand,
Never forget, hope will take you by the hand.

Sam Iles (11)
Holymead Junior School

My Cat

My cat sleeps the day away
She could sleep until May.
Her name is Poppy
And she's ever so soppy!

Her favourite thing to do is eat
And she always cleans her furry little feet.
She looks like a hairy little ball
But when she stretches she's very tall.

Anna Yeatman (10)
Holymead Junior School

The Tree Man

(Inspired by a painting of The Tree Man)

The tree man wails in the gale,
He sways and shudders in the frozen forest.
There is no life, only death and darkness.
The life is leaving him, it flows away like a river.
The tree man sees the light of Heaven.
He plods heavily towards the gateway.
The stairs are there, steep and narrow.
He tries to climb them.
He is frozen.
He stands, his head down.
No one will help him.
He is *alone.*

Elliot Mills
Holymead Junior School

My Dog

My dog's got a black, shiny nose
My dog eats my slippers
My dog gives me wet doggy kisses
My dog doesn't like cats
My dog's old but young at heart.
I love my dog.
I love him lots!

Natasha Joslin (11)
Holymead Junior School

My Magic Box!

(Based on 'Magic Box' by Kit Wright)

I will put into my box . . .
Millions of shiny, black horses
All animals, kind, mean, rough and tough
Happy things all over the world.

I will put into my box . . .
Silky snakes standing on stallions
Musical monkeys bound to go crazy
A wonderful brass band that can teach me to play.

I will put into my box . . .
Everlasting money for the RSPCA
Beautiful flowers, all different colours
Exmoor with all Exmoor ponies.

I will put into my box . . .
Everyone happy
Everybody's cheerful smiles
My box is made of metal with sparkles glistening all over.

I will put into my box . . .
My black, cuddly dog Mylo
My fluffy, cheeky pony Catkin
My family, I know they're always there!
Hopefully they won't mind being shoved in a box!

Alice Riddiford (9)
North Road CP School

Dalmatians!

Dalmatians, Dalmatians,
Cute little pups,
Dalmatians, Dalmatians,
Drink out of cups,
Dalmatians, Dalmatians,
Run in the sea,
Dalmatians, Dalmatians,
All love me!

Rebekah Harvey (10)
North Road CP School

My Magic Box

(Based on 'Magic Box' by Kit Wright)

I will put into my box . . .
A golden lion with a furry mane
Shiny crystals from a giant rock
A snowy-white polar bear with a smile.

I will put into my box . . .
A bright pink flamingo
My family's laughter.

I will put into my box . . .
A lime-green plant
A moon, sky-white vase
And hope.

My box is fashioned from wood
Ice-blue on the outside with stars
Golden money for the hinges
And sparkling silver inside.

Joanne Boulton (9)
North Road CP School

Dolphins

D ancing, prancing dolphins
O nward they go to end their journey
L iving in the sea
P laying with such beauty and elegance
H iding in the waves
I n such a panic
N arwhal
S traight ahead

Oh! No!

Paige Walters (9)
North Road CP School

Home Sweet Home?

Beth's sad,
Cats are mad,
Fish a-tipping,
Tap a-dripping,
Babies yelling,
Penny telling,
Vacuum blaring,
Carpet tearing,
Grandpa's boring,
Dad's snoring,
Children playing,
Sitter saying,
'Here comes Mum,
Tina's chum.'
Pineapple cube in the hamster's tube,
How full!

Molly Jenkins (9)
North Road CP School

The Tree

The tree is tall
Brown and thin.

The tree is warm
With squirrels in.

The tree has
Chicks in its arms.

The tree is
Swaying in the wind.

Sophie Bolton (9)
North Road CP School

Magic Box

(Based on 'Magic Box' by Kit Wright)

I will put into my box . . .
A time machine so you can travel to the good times.

I will put into my box . . .
A snowdrop of the lovely day in spring.

I will put into my box . . .
Some of my wonderful, brilliant friends
So I know they're always there for me.

I will put into my box . . .
A cow playing noughts and crosses
So when I'm down I can have a laugh.

I will put into my box . . .
Snowy mountains all glittery and sweet.

I will put into my box . . .
A talking toilet.

I will put into my box . . .
A flying pig on a broomstick.

Charlotte Anne Brankin (9)
North Road CP School

Cats

Cats are:
    Cool
Cats are:
    Mischievous
Cats are:
    Friendly
Cats are:
    Hunters in the house
Cats, cats, everywhere.

Nathalie Moore (10)
North Road CP School

My Magic Box

(Based on 'Magic Box' by Kit Wright)

I will put into my box . . .
My mum's magical jewellery from a long time ago
I will put a red, rosy poppy in
To think of all the people that have died in the war
I will put France in my box
When I was 9 my dad used to go a long way to France
To work on an aeroplane.

I will put in my box . . .
My friends Natasha and Paige to remind me of the time at school
When we met each other
My funky friendship bracelets from school
Then summer and winter to remind me of the seasons.

I will put in my box . . .
My loveable family because I love them so much
My bedroom with all of the things I used to cuddle up to
When I was little.

My magic box is made of . . .
Gold, silver and bronze
The hinges are fluffy, purple feathers
With colourful crystals on the box
Which makes it fantastic to look at.

Beth Staley (10)
North Road CP School

The Playground I'm In!

Come and see the playground of your dreams
Tall swings, small slides
Laughing kids, crying kids
Lovely teachers, loud teachers
In the end I hope you like my playground.

Catherine Brankin (10)
North Road CP School

Poems

Poems can be short
Poems can be sweet
Poems can be about apples
That are crunchy to eat

Poems can be funny
Poems can be long
Poems can be sad and
Read like a song!

Katie Gowen (11)
North Road CP School

Summer

Summer is relaxing
Summer is creating
Summer is hot
Summer is fun
Summer is brill
Summer is quiet
Summer is sunny
Summer is cool
Summer is exciting.

Oliver Pagington (10)
North Road CP School

Friends Forever

Friends, friends, how good they can be
Friends, friends, the best they can be
Friends, friends, best, best friends
Friends, friends forever and ever.

Ryan Mackereth (9)
North Road CP School

My Box

(Based on 'Magic Box' by Kit Wright)

I will put in my box . . .
Some happiness and joy
And some of my special toys

I will put in my box . . .
Some magic if I need something
And some of my best friends

I will put in my box . . .
Something that reminds me of the seasons
A drop of the crystal-blue sea

I will put in my box . . .
A feather from a golden eagle
And the first snowdrop of spring

I will put in my box . . .
Money for the RSPCA for all of the animals
And a crystal piece of ice.

Zoe Potts (10)
North Road CP School

Weather

Weather, weather, you are so great.
How you make it so dark for when I need to sleep.
Then it is so very light and bright for me to see.

Weather, weather
You can be very cold and wet
Which I need to wear my hat and coat.
I love to play in the white stuff which is snow.

Weather, weather
When you are so hot it is so great.
That is when I play the best.
I play in my swimming pool
And eat ice cream and ice lollies all day long.

Weather, weather.

Jessica Davey (7)
Novers Lane Junior School

Wishing

I wish I was in Egypt
I would go across the desert
I'd be a frog so I'd go and be the greatest thing
I would go to pirates and say, 'Parlez'
I could be a businessman
Or build special things and develop buildings around the world
I could be the richest man with all the money in the world
But I'll stay me for now.

Luke Sheehan (9)
Novers Lane Junior School

Boys

Boys smell, they're really cruel,
They enjoy playing football.
Boys and girls don't get along,
My cousin thinks he's really strong!

Boys, boys sometimes are crazy
They can also be quite lazy.
I'm glad I'm not a boy
I'm a girl.

Chelsea Cox (8)
Novers Lane Junior School

De More De Merrier

(Based on a poem by Opal Palmer Adisa)

Sitting in my bedroom watching TV
People running past, laughing and joking
I am feeling very sad and lonely
My doorbell or phone is not ringing at all
Why doesn't anyone want to call up for me?

Lauren Travanti (9)
Novers Lane Junior School

For A Little Friendship

(Based on a poem by Jarostav Vrchlicky)

For a little friendship
I would stand on nails.
I would swim across the ocean
For a little friendship.
At times like this
I wish there was a friendship ship.
I would do the biggest jump ever.
I would buy them any presents
The best in the whole wide world
For a little friendship.

Jack Bushby (9)
Novers Lane Junior School

Time

(Based on a poem by Bruce Lansky)

Telling people not to walk,
Telling dogs not to bark,
Telling children not to talk,
Telling light to save the dark.

Telling cats not to scratch,
Telling parents not to sigh,
Telling chicks not to hatch,
Telling animals not to die.

Toni Pring (8)
Novers Lane Junior School

Rain

Swimming down the hill
Drumming on the dustbin
Clapping on the window
Shining on the lamp post
Splashing on the pavement.

Billy-Joe Wring (8)
Novers Lane Junior School

My Brother

My brother is crazy
My mum would say it's because he's twelve
I would say it's because he's . . . well . . .
I wouldn't like to say

My brother is an alien
He looks like one
He walks like one
He has got to be an alien

My brother is a piglet
He oinks like one
He eats like one
He has got to be a piglet

Even if my brother is crazy
Or an alien
Even a piglet
I still love my brother.

Tatiyanna Knight (9)
Novers Lane Junior School

Teddy Bear

Teddy bear, I love you
I would cuddle you all day
With your cute face.

Teddy bear, I love you
I would look at you all day
With your soft tummy.

Teddy bear, I love you
I would do anything for you
With your arms and legs.

Teddy bear, stay with me.

Carla Griffin (9)
Novers Lane Junior School

The Moon

In the deep darkness of the night
A friendly eye looks down on us
Guarding and guiding us
Until the beaming sun rises and pushes it away.

In the deep darkness of the night
Something shiny as a jewel looks down on us
Until the beaming sun rises and takes over.

Melissa Smithers (8)
Novers Lane Junior School

The Moon

The moon follows us
Up in the sky
It goes as slow as a snail
And it looks like cheese pie.

The moon looks like a banana,
It is silver and hairy
And big
And fat.

James Whittaker (9)
Novers Lane Junior School

People And Animals

People are great,
People are fun,
Never thick,
Never dumb.

Animals are pretty,
Animals are cute,
They will be noisy
If you play the flute.

Jenny Hill (8)
Novers Lane Junior School

My Pet

You'll never guess my pet
He has great beady eyes
He loves to swim in water
And munching on flies.

You'll never guess my pet
Oh no! He's escaped from his cage
I spotted him there on the paper
Oh no! He peed on my homework page.

You'll never guess my pet
With his cage so clean
My mum doesn't like him
She thinks he's very mean.

You'll never guess my pet
He's jumped down the bog
I quickly got him back again
The little cheeky frog.

Jiorgia Fitton (11)
Novers Lane Junior School

De More De Merrier

(Based on a poem by Opal Palmer Adisa)

Sitting on the sofa.
Looking at the fireplace.
Watching pop music.
Wanting my mum and dad
But at home alone.
No sister.
No mum.
No dad.
Not even a brother to talk to.
How do you feel?
Upset?

Katie Willett (9)
Novers Lane Junior School

As We Speak

As we speak we are missing Dawson's Creek.
As we speak someone is packing and leaving.
As we speak everything is changing around us.
As we speak we don't realise what we are saying.
As we speak we all sound different to others.

As we speak we don't know what others are thinking about.
As we speak we get older and older.

As we speak we are not calling our friends.
As we speak everyone disappears.

Samantha Hunt (9)
Novers Lane Junior School

Holiday

I went on holiday
Far, far away.
It was called Sandy Glade
On a little bay.
The sun shone hot and bright
I could see everything in my sight.
The sea was a sparkling blue
The sand looked so soft and new.

Skye Lewis (8)
Novers Lane Junior School

The Moon

The moon is a big snowball,
It follows us across the sky,
And plays hide-and-seek in the night sky.
The moon is a big monster in the sky,
It likes to play games with me,
And as it moves through the clouds,
It peeps and creeps.

Hollie Christian (8)
Novers Lane Junior School

A Waste Of Time

(Based on a poem by Bruce Lansky)

Telling children not to fight;
Telling birds not to sing;
Telling spiders not to fright;
Telling phones not to ring.

Telling bears not to roar;
Telling beetles not to scurry;
Telling people not to snore;
Telling mums not to worry.

Telling dads not to smoke;
Telling cats not to chase rats;
Telling friends a good joke;
Telling ladies not to wear hats.

Jordan Porter (9)
Novers Lane Junior School

The Moon

The moon is like a button,
Shining so bright,
Running round the world,
Day and night.

The moon is like an eye,
Watching where you go,
It's like people,
Saying hello!

The moon is like a football,
Racing after you,
Watching where you are,
And watching what you do.

Tamara Eddy (9)
Novers Lane Junior School

A Waste Of Time

(Based on a poem by Bruce Lansky)

Telling a mouse to be tall
Telling school not to be real
Telling children not to fall
Telling people not to make a deal

Telling people not to have mail
Telling scientists not to be smart
Telling children to go to Hell
Telling dogs not to have a heart

Telling ducks not to waddle
Telling children not to be small
Telling people not to model
Telling me not to go in the hall

Telling people not to swim
Telling babies not to cry
Telling people not to grin
Telling kids don't be shy

Telling people not to sing
Telling bubbles not to pop
Telling bees not to sting
Telling children not to hop.

Kealy Lea (9)
Novers Lane Junior School

Lauren Day

L oves to play
A lways there, never away.
U nder my skin is a loving heart,
R ight up there on a number one chart.
E ven when I'm feeling down,
N ever a worry, never a frown.

D irt is my thing, I'm always messy,
A nd my favourite chips are even Aunt Bessie,
Y ou'll always spot me because I'm Lauren Day.

Lauren Day (8)
Novers Lane Junior School

Football Training

Football training
Got to get ready
Hope it's not raining
Because I can't play

Put my boots on
Tie up the laces
Run onto the pitch
Passing the ball different places
G . . . o . . . a . . . l!

Ben Llewellyn (8)
Novers Lane Junior School

My Bed!

We sleep in beds
All nice and snug
We spill our hot chocolate
That was in a mug.

'This is my bed,' said a bird
With no 'tweet, tweet'
Up high in a tree
With eggs of joy
Daddy out searching
For a long-lost toy.
Scattering for a pin
When her son is out
For when he falls in a bin.

'This is my bed,' said a big, tough bear
With a loud roar.
In a dusty cave
All dirty and cold
Then all my good food
Turned into gold.
If people come to me
I think, *who are they*
And who is he?

Dogs, cats, fish
Hamsters and mouses
All these animals
Live in houses.

The seals in a glass-green sea
Where do all the other animals live?
Please tell me.

Taylor Ann Morgan (9)
Novers Lane Junior School

I Feel Sad

(Based on a poem by Opal Palmer Adisa)

Sitting in the park
Looking at the tree
Watching the people playing
Wanting to play with my friends
But in the park on my own
No fish
No dogs
No brother
Not even a sister to talk to
I feel sad.

Kayley Grist (9)
Novers Lane Junior School

The Firework Night

Sparklers and cartwheels
And also bonfires
It's firework night
We are all dressed up
But my skirt is fairly tight

Everyone is dressed
Dressed very well
When the party is over
We'll have lots of stories to tell.

Roxanne Gregory (9)
Novers Lane Junior School

Waterfall

W aterfalls are very fast flowing
A ll the water flashing and dashing through the stream
T umbling water falling over the waterfall edge
E stuaries meet the sea that's why they're called estuaries
R ushing rivers take rocks and branches with them
F rogs jumping down the stream
A nd underneath the water it is all dirty
L ovely rivers make the world a better place
L owering and rising rivers.

Harvey Arnold (9)
Oldbury-On-Severn Primary School

Springtime

Springtime is my favourite time of year.
The lambs are born and they're leaping everywhere.
The kittens are trying to open their eyes
And the foals are crying to their mums all night.
The birds are cheeping in the high up sky.
The flowers all bloom in front of me.
This is why I love springtime.

Emily Jessop (11)
Oldbury-On-Severn Primary School

Snowfall

S wirling snowflakes falling
N othing to see but white
O pen the door to have a look
W inter days are always cold
F lakes of snow fall silently
A ll wrapped up warm
L isten to the children playing
L ook someone's made a snowman.

Cameron Proctor (11)
Oldbury-On-Severn Primary School

Frostbite

F reezing fingers
R obins fly around
O n top of my home is a blanket of snow
S now crunches under your feet
T eeth chatter with the cold winds
B itter and cold
I cicles hang like daggers
T rees sprinkled with snowdrops
E veryone comes out for snowball fights.

Joe Porter (11)
Oldbury-On-Severn Primary School

Snowfall

S now that glints in the sun,
N orway where it's always cold,
O ld toboggans that whizz down hills,
W inds that make avalanches,
F lakes of snow that fall,
A lways fun to roll in,
L aughter when snowballs are thrown
L ots of fun while it lasts.

Daniel Bond (10)
Oldbury-On-Severn Primary School

Sadness

Sadness is grey as the rainclouds
Sadness sounds like a drip of your tears,
Sadness looks like a bad memory,
Sadness tastes like your blood when you die,
Sadness feels like you want to go to sleep forever,
Sadness reminds me of your heart stopping beating!

Harry Collin (10)
Oldbury-On-Severn Primary School

Winter Stars

The bright stars shoot by!
They twinkle up in the sky
The snow twinkles on the stars
It gently falls on the cars
Snowflakes fall to the ground
They twizzle, twizzle all around
The colour changes in a cloud
It's coming out to shout aloud
The frosty water twinkles blue
It's there for you
The stars are a good sight to see
The snow twinkles just right for me.

Carys Harvey (9)
Oldbury-On-Severn Primary School

Snowdrop

S lippery ice makes people slide.
N asty blizzard blazes over people and obstacles.
O ther Christmas still to come.
W inter cold and icy
D rizzles of rain in-between
R apid blizzards ripping rooftops off.
O bjects go spinning on the roads.
P olice being called out for emergencies.

Alex Gaston (10)
Oldbury-On-Severn Primary School

I Am A Rosebud

I am a cheeky monkey
Swinging from tree to tree
I am a rosebud blossoming in the sun
I am a bouncing beanbag, jolly and cheerful,
I am a motorist zooming in the wind
I am the colour yellow, sunny and bright
I am as sweet as sugar,
I am the Eiffel Tower, tall and proud.

Amy Fillingham (10)
St Anne's Park Primary School

I Wanna Be A Superstar

I wanna be a superstar
I wanna drive a racing car
I wanna join the royal part
I wanna own a posh cart
I wanna lotta swimming pools
I wanna name that's really cool
I wanna lotta private bars
I wanna be a superstar.

Clariss Morgan (10)
St Anne's Park Primary School

I Am Sherbet

I am a fox clever as can be,
I am a tree tall as can be,
I am a comfy sofa, soft and relaxed,
I am a Ferrari, funky and fast,
I am blue, cool and calm,
I am sherbet, sour and sharp!

Jessy Waller (10)
St Anne's Park Primary School

The Sound Collector

(Inspired by 'The Sound Collector' by Roger McGough)

Someone phoned this morning
She didn't say her name
Left us only with silence
So nothing is the same.

Phones ringing all the time
The creaking of the stairs
The noise comes from an echo
Because of the banging on the concrete stairs.

The doors banging open
Toasters popping up fast
The tables scratching the floor
Children laughing from the past

Pens scratching the whiteboard
Also children crying
Children bashing things up
None of the children lying.

Yvette Rees (9)
St Anne's Park Primary School

I Wanna Be A Superstar

I wanna drive a massive car.
I wanna join the lotto fame.
I wanna own a private game.
I wanna lotta cool spotlights.
I wanna name that's up in lights.
I wanna lotta private bars.
I wanna be a superstar.
I wanna wear a mini skirt.
I wanna jump in lovely dirt.

Kelly Courtney (10)
St Anne's Park Primary School

I Am . . .

I am a joker funny as ever,
I am water hot or cold,
I am a bouncy castle bouncy and fun,
I am a balloon waiting to be popped,
I am a flower beautiful and bright,
I am a dinosaur furious and angry
I am as sweet as sugar,
I am also as sour as sherbet.

Abigail Wren (10)
St Anne's Park Primary School

Green Creeper

Lily leaper
Green creeper
Yellow belly
Big and smelly
Big jumper
Fish thumper
Big eyes
Likes flies.

Chloe Johnson (11)
St Anne's Park Primary School

Weston

Slow donkeys strolling along the sand
Seagulls are squawking almost laughing
Hot curry dripping on my chips
Smelling the sharp salt air hit my nose
Feeling the sand rushing
Through my fingers.

Ashley Hutchison (10)
St Anne's Park Primary School

The Sound Collector

(Based on 'The Sound Collector' by Roger McGough)

An old man came this morning
Got to work right away
Put sounds in a big bag
He was dressed in black and grey.

The ringing of the school bell
The sweeping of a brush
The moaning of a teacher
The children in a rush.

The flushing of the toilet
The slamming of a book
The scraping of the pushchairs
Coats swishing on a hook.

The creaking of the blue door
The wiping of a cloth
The stamping in the hallway
Little children's coughs.

A stranger called this morning
He didn't leave his name
He left us only silence
Life will never be the same.

Alexandra Mlewa (9)
St Anne's Park Primary School

The Sound Collector

(Inspired by 'The Sound Collector' by Roger McGough)

The clicking of the doorknob
The whooshing of the flush
The rustling of the hairbrush
The laugh of the teachers
The crunching of the leaves
The tweeting of the bird
The buzzing of the bees.

Jack Hodges (9)
Two Mile Hill Junior School

My Birthday Surprise

I am surprised about my present
Like a chair is shocked of snapping
Like a clock is gobsmacked by a powercut
Like a poster is dismayed by rainfall
Like a ruler is astonished of breaking
Like a bat is amazed of hitting
I am surprised about my present.

Daniel Cotton (11)
Two Mile Hill Junior School

Sound In School

The echoing of the hall
The bouncing of the ball
Children saying, 'What a score'
The banging of a door
Children saying, 'What a goal'
The ball banging on the wall.

Carla Taylor (10)
Two Mile Hill Junior School

A Robber Causes Crime!

A robber causes crime
Spends life in jail to pass time
He is let free
But one more time
He'll be back in jail to pass time.

Sophie Bennett (10)
Two Mile Hill Junior School

The School Sound Collector
(Inspired by 'The Sound Collector' by Roger McGough)

The banging of the doors
The bashing of the books
The twisting of the bottletops
The squeaking of the hooks.

The snapping of rulers
The crunching of leaves
The shouting of the teachers
The swaying of the trees.

The scratching of the pencils
The crunching of the sharpener
The clashing of the chairs
The swishing of the blinds.

Paige Webb (10)
Two Mile Hill Junior School

The School Sound Collector
(Inspired by 'The Sound Collector' by Roger McGough)

The singing of the children
The crashing of the door
The kicking of footballs
The squeaking of the floor.

The shouting of the children
The laughing of a child
The chatting of a teacher
Some child's gone wild.

The buzzing of a computer
There's some left on the floor
Our teacher's shouting
I need more, more, more.

Ruby Batt (10)
Two Mile Hill Junior School

Colours

Colours are everywhere
The yellow sun
The blue sea
The green leaves
Colours are everywhere
The white clouds
The orange tigers
The black rhinos
Colours are everywhere
The golden eagle
The clear rain
The grey elephant
Colours are everywhere
The brown wood
The peach beach
And the most colourful rainbow in the world
Colours are all over the world!

Nadim Ahmed (10)
Two Mile Hill Junior School

The School Sound Collector

(Inspired by 'The Sound Collector' by Roger McGough)

The sign of the people laughing
The tapping of some feet
The squeaking of a pen
The teachers having a meet
The bouncing of a football
The shouting of the football team
The screaming of the children
The cheering of a football team.

Megan Davies (9)
Two Mile Hill Junior School

Weather

Snow is cool
Snow is fun
It melts in the sun
Make a snowball
Slip, slide and fall
Snow is good
Snow is great
When you play you can't hate.

Rain is bad
Rain isn't fun
It keeps away the cool sun
Make a splash
Splish splash fall with a crash
Rain isn't good
Rain isn't great
You really can hate

The sun is cool
The sun is fun
Let's go out and play with the sun
Make a castle made of sand
Fall over and have a hard land
The sun is good
The sun is great
You just can't hate!

Sam Bracey (9)
Two Mile Hill Junior School

Surprised

I am surprised about Christmas
Like a monkey amazed about bananas
Like a fish is gobsmacked by a shark
Like a mouse is shocked by cheese
Like a library is flabbergasted by books
Like a deer is astounded by a lion
I am surprised about Christmas.

Caroline Parry (10)
Two Mile Hill Junior School

Why Should We Look After The World?

Why should we look after the world?
To keep it nice and clean
To stop nasty pollution
Like car's gasoline.

Loads of cans and litter
Scattered on the street
Some foods are bitter
Some just stay a seed.

Loads of people harmless
Even little kids too
Loads of people dirty and muddy
And nowhere to go to the loo.

The sea is like you and me
But how can you keep it nice and clean?
To stop an enemy submarine
To stop one of our ships sinking!

Sam Ryan (11)
Two Mile Hill Junior School

Rainforest

The snapping of the crocodile
The flying of the bird
The flowing of the river
The jumping of the ants.

The sucking of the frog
The tweeting of the bird
The hanging of the monkey
The hissing of the snake.

The sound is wonderful.

Shaun Trott (9)
Two Mile Hill Junior School

Leave Me Alone!

Stop this bullying, stop it now
There are probably bullies out now on the prowl
Whacking and scratching and hitting galore
So you better stop In the name of the law.
If there are bullies and you don't know what to do
Then tell a friend who is close to you
Don't be a bully yourself, because you think it's cool
Tell somebody that you know from school
Just think how sad you can make them feel
If you've got a problem you should keep it real
So don't bully people over one silly thing
And make them unhappy when they hear that bell ring.

Chloe Depledge (9)
Two Mile Hill Junior School

Bullying! Our Rap

I was bullied once
Now I'm a bully too
They took it out on me
So I'll take it out on you.

So don't be in the gang
Just because it's cool
You will soon get caught
By a teacher at school.

So if you're bullied
Look for someone with a blue band
Tell them your problems
And they'll give you a hand.
So stop it, it's wrong!

Kobi Cole (10), Kayleigh Evans & Alex Sheppard (11)
Two Mile Hill Junior School

The School Sound Collector

(Inspired by 'The Sound Collector' by Roger McGough)

The thumping of the footsteps
The banging of the doors
The whispering of the children
The creaking of the floors.

The shouting of the teachers
The children working hard
The laughing of the children
The teacher signing a card.

The squeaking of whiteboard pens
The music in the hall
The singing of the children
The teacher answering a phone call.

Natalie Earle (9)
Two Mile Hill Junior School

The School Sound Collector

(Inspired by 'The Sound Collector' by Roger McGough)

The screaming of the children
The music of the hall
The munching of the sandwiches
The bouncing of the ball.

The kicking of the football
The squeaking on the whiteboard
The kids going to the book stall
The snapping of the pencils
The ringing of the bell
The snapping of the rulers
The banging of the door.

Aaron Comer (9)
Two Mile Hill Junior School

The Sound Collector

(Inspired by 'The Sound Collector' by Roger McGough)

The laughing of the teachers
The thudding of the ball
The rusting of the whiteboards
The echo of the hall.

The snapping of the rulers
The kicking of the leaves
The banging of the doors
The buzzing of the bees.

The screaming of the children
The whistling of the trees
The bouncing of the ball
The buzzing of the bees.

Jake Morris (10)
Two Mile Hill Junior School

The School Sound Collector

(Inspired by 'The Sound Collector' by Roger McGough)

The ringing of the bell
The squeaking of the door
The teachers screaming
The children walking on the class floor.

The tapping of the pencil
The squeaking of the chair
The screaming on the playground
The girls messing with their hair.

Olivia Silvestre (9)
Two Mile Hill Junior School

Bullying

Stop this bullying, stop it now
There are probably bullies out on the prowl,
Walking and scratching and hitting galore
So you'd better stop, in the name of the law.

If there's a bully and you don't know what to do
Tell a friend that is close to you,
Then they will help you,
They will know just what to do.

Kicking and spitting and shouting some more
Telling tales and saying, 'No more!'

Lauren Dennis (9)
Two Mile Hill Junior School

Bullies

B ullies bother
U seless to
L ittle really
L ike to annoy you
I t is a horrible and nasty thing to do
E liminate the bully from your life
S o tell someone and they can help you!

Shannon Davies (11)
Two Mile Hill Junior School

Joyful Poem

I am excited about playing ball
Like a cat is pleased to be stroked
Like a flower is jolly in the rain
Like a car is happy to have a car wash
Like a book is content to be read
Like a pen is joyful to be used
I am excited playing ball.

Saqib Naeem (10)
Two Mile Hill Junior School

My Friends

My friends are the most important things to me
And even though we disagree
We guarantee that we will be the best that we could be
Because my friends are part of my family

They are a bright light shining down
They are an ever smiling clown
Who never let's me frown
Even when I've had a breakdown

They make me laugh and sometimes cry
And they will always make me deny
That they are right and I am wrong
But they always make me feel as if I belong with them

My friends always have the power over me
And even though we disagree
Whether a he or she
They are part of my family tree.

Leanne Bond (11)
Two Mile Hill Junior School

I Am Sad

I am sad about breaking the window
Like a pencil is down about going down
Like a chocolate bar is disappointed about melting
Like a piece of paper is moody about being cut
Like a chair is displeased about being farted on
Like a light upset about getting changed
Like a blind left lonely in a classroom
Like a gloomy campfire on a rainy day
I am sad about breaking the window.

Jack Handley (9)
Two Mile Hill Junior School

Crocodile

Its teeth are sharp
Its claws are deadly
Its tail is wiggly as a snake
Its nose is big
Its colour is green
Its feet are gleaming
Beware the crocodile
Swimming in the Nile.

Kane Crouch (9)
Two Mile Hill Junior School

Fear To Fear

I am scared of spiders
Like a hamster is worried of a cage
Like a bottle is petrified of mouths
Like a zoo animal is scared of bars
Like a bath is terrified of water
I am scared of a spider.

Denise Morgan (10)
Two Mile Hill Junior School

I Am Scared Of

I am scared of a bee!
Like a floor is petrified of a mop!
Like a chair is horrified of a bottom!
Like a carpet is frightened of a vacuum
Like a lead is anxious of a sharpener!
I am scared of a bee!

Samuel Tompkins (11)
Two Mile Hill Junior School

What Is What?

What is green? Green is the grass
What is orange? Orange is an orange
What is blue? Blue is the sky where the rain drops
What is a sun? A sun is a round ball
What is a bonfire? A bonfire is a rocket that blows up in the sky
What is a snake? A snake is an animal that eats you up in one gulp
What is red? Red is a rose
What is brown? Brown is a coconut, coconuts are round like a football
What is a motorbike? A motorbike is a large, heavy bicycle with
                                              an engine
What is a mouse? A mouse is a small furry animal with a long tail
What is a moth? A moth is an insect like a butterfly that flies
                                           around at night
What is an octopus? An octopus is a sea creature with eight tentacles.
What? What? What?

Mohamed Abdiaziz (10)
Two Mile Hill Junior School

Spy

They call me spy
And I know why
You'll see me on the stairs
So they will walk up in pairs
I will see them with my eye
Then they wave and say, 'Hi.'

I lean on the wall
To watch over them all
I stand there and miss my play
Near the doorway is where I stay
The purpose of my duty call
Is to make sure no one falls.

Emma Hine (11)
Two Mile Hill Junior School

I Am Scared Of The Dark

I am scared of the dark
Like a crisp wrapper is scared of a bin
Like a pencil is nervous of paper
Like a pen is nervous of a board
Like a hamster is terrified of a cage
Like a car is terrified of the road
Like a chair is scared of the floor
Like a toothbrush is horrified of teeth
Like a dog is scared of a cat.

Lucy Callaghan (10)
Two Mile Hill Junior School

I Am Scared

I am scared of spiders
Like a book is nervous of getting shut
Like a toothbrush is terrified of my teeth
Like a cake is scared of getting eaten
Like a present is fearful of getting unwrapped
Like a tap is petrified of getting turned off
I am scared of spiders.

Shannon Camreon (9)
Two Mile Hill Junior School

Spiderphobia

I'm scared of spiders
Like a sheep's wool is nervous of a shearer
Like an ice cube is petrified of the sun
Like vines are terrified of Tarzan!
Like the carpet is frightened of being pulled up
I'm scared of spiders.

Jade Montagna-Malcolm (9)
Two Mile Hill Junior School

The Pond Monster

I can't go near the pond in the park
Or I'll get eaten by a kid eating lark
Many times I wish to go
Not when I'm near by my brother though
He warned me over and over again
My sister didn't listen then
She fell in one windy day
Nothing was left but a pile of hay
I never knew I had a sister
But some days I hear a gentle whisper
Warning me not to go near the pond
How one day she had been conned
To walk into the swirling pool
And how it would feel so very cool
But I still wonder whether one day
He told me that just to play
When I ask him he turns a blind eye
And how not to tell Mum or she might cry
I asked Mum what was a lark
She replied, 'Not as scary as a shark'
But still I ask if it's true
I'm not sure - are you?

Samantha Gould (11)
Two Mile Hill Junior School

Arachnophobia

I'm scared of spiders
Like water is scared of a freezer
Like fire is intimidated of being put out
Like a snooker ball is petrified of the cue
Like a book is terrified of being shut
I'm scared of spiders.

Craig Kemp (11)
Two Mile Hill Junior School

The Sound Snatcher

(Based on 'The Sound Collector' by Roger McGough)

A stranger in school this morning
Dressed in baggy rags
He came to school to nick some sounds
And put them in some bags

He even nicked Mr Tong's voice (head)
And everyone was happy
But then we got surprised
And returned as a happy chappy

The screaming of the teacher
The sound of kids crying
The people that were missed
The sound of pigeons dying

The sound of people on the street
The sound of clip-clop on your feet
The sound of a ball on the street
The sound of music's beat

The sounds of pencils writing
The sound of clocks ticking
The sound of balls being thrown
The sound of people kicking

The sound of people working
The sound of people doing art
The sound of pencils moving
The sound of people's fluffs

The sound of us singing
The sound of the caretaker's dog
The sound of the bell
The sound of the bog.

Rikki Maine (10)
Two Mile Hill Junior School

Teachers Of Our Time

Here are teachers and their features

Miss Simpson has a major thing on wigs
She dances in the sun all day long
With hippy songs
She is da best and is better than da rest.

Miss Global is a mado
Belly button disaster
Tattoo wearer jocko
Nose picker master
And is the wackiest teacher of all time.

Mr Marble is a rolling disaster
Platted hair is a matter
Smells like beer
Likes to shoot deer
That's a disaster.

Mr Spoon
He is up to the moon
He is 7 foot tall as is a giant balloon
And he is exactly like a baboon
That's Mr Spoon.

Lewis Trott (10)
Two Mile Hill Junior School

Ghostaphobia

I am scared of ghosts
Like a bottle is petrified of lips
Like water is horrified of a bath
Like a ball is fearful of a foot
Like a hamster is anxious of a cage
I am scared of ghosts.

Tayler Withey (9)
Two Mile Hill Junior School

A Stranger In School

(Inspired by 'The Sound Collector' by Roger McGough)

A stranger in school this morning
Dressed in blue and black
Put every sound into a bag
And never brought them back

The banging of the blinds
The tapping of the keyboard
The clatter of a chair
The sound of an award

The rustling of paper
The voice of Miss Cuthbert
The flapping of a book
The children shouting about stuff

The sound of a marker
The tapping of a pencil
The children laughing
The sound of a stencil

The clicking of a clock
The ticking of a switch
The sound of cutting scissors
The boys playing football on a football pitch

The sound of the sink
Boys singing football songs
Girls scraping pencils
Teachers eating bonbons.

Katie Williams (10)
Two Mile Hill Junior School

Teachers

Teachers are mad
They can be bad
Teachers cane
Teachers give pain
Teach teach
Teachers

Teacher's big
Teacher's small
Mad, mad
Teachers

Teachers shout
Teachers pout
Mad, mad
Teachers

Teachers shout
Teachers pout
Strict
Strict
Teachers.

Jordan Blake (11)
Two Mile Hill Junior School

Baaphobia

I am scared of sheep
Like a nail is petrified of a hammer
Like a fire fears a bucket of water
Like a chair is horrified of a bottom
Like a pencil is nervous around a sharpener
Like your teeth are scared of sweets.

I am scared of sheep.

Shane Baker (11)
Two Mile Hill Junior School

My Pet

I have a pet called Dave
He can sing, dance and shave
He has his own kite
He ends up having a fight
And eats everything in sight

I have a pet called Mark
Who thinks he is a shark
He loves the sea
He bites nobody but me
And he only drinks tea

I have a pet called Steve
And he will only believe
That the world is blue
Which isn't true
And that there is only one of you

I have a pet called Mary
Who thinks she is always scary
She has a big heart
She likes being called sweetheart
And likes looking at art.

Georgia Batt (9)
Two Mile Hill Junior School

I Am Scared Of Spiders

I am scared of spiders
Like a dirty plate is nervous of hot water
Like a cake is horrified of being eaten
Like a text is petrified of being deleted
Like a present is dismayed at being unwrapped
Like a door is anxious of being slammed
I am scared of spiders.

Jeelendra Singh (10)
Two Mile Hill Junior School

The Family From Springfield

Homer is the best
He's better than all the rest

Marge is his wife
He loves his life

Bart is the worst
But Homer would burst

With Maggie sucking her dummy
She always wants her mummy

Lisa is the best in the school
She always sings in the hall

Bart has a friend called Millhouse
They always get in trouble

Marge has no friends
But Homer drives her round the bend

Lisa has some friends
But she hasn't got the trend

Maggie met Simon Cowell
But he said 'You haven't got the talent'

Homer's got a best friend called Barney
But he's always on the beer

This is the family from Springfield
Maybe the best in the world!

Bradley Pearce (11)
Two Mile Hill Junior School

My Phobia

I am scared of homework
Like a piece of paper is petrified of a pencil
Like a plate is frightened of a chip
Like a worm is terrified of a magpie
I am scared of homework.

Kimberley Jones (9)
Two Mile Hill Junior School

Friends

All my friends are very funny
When they are around it is so sunny

My friends are always kind
Our fun and laughter can never be timed

We have a laugh as we play
We gossip each and every day

It's better when you have a good friend
Even if they may drive you round the bend

We will be all best friends
Till the very end!

Melissa Hooper (11)
Two Mile Hill Junior School

Why Dad?

Why are roses red, Dad?
Why is the grass green?
Why do we have numbers, Dad?
I really want to know!
Why are my eyes brown, Dad?
Why is the sky blue?
Why aren't you listening, Dad?
I want to speak to you
Why are stars small, Dad?
Why is snow white?
Why do people talk, Dad?
Why? Why? Why?

Demi Heaven (10)
Two Mile Hill Junior School

Rainforest Terrors

When you venture into a rainforest
Who knows what you might find
Bearded pigs, tapirs, even a chimpanzee
Creeping, crawling mysterious things
Lurking beneath your feet
You might even discover a type of flying frogs
Or singing honeybees!

When things get dark and dingy
When the clouds start to leek
Where will you go?
When parrots take the banana leaves
And termites steel all the trees
Animals snug and dry
Your feet overtaken by fungi
As you start to
Count sheep
Twiddle your thumbs
Reading your book for the 20th time
Well as you're stranded in the rainforest
Remember you're not alone!

The parrots are squawking
The monkeys are squealing
But you are starting to go insane
Barely coping with the rainforest terrors!

On the tree trunks you sit and wait
For a forest frog
To leap and bound through the ferns
But secretly it's another rainforest terror
Waiting for its prey
Be warned that it might be you!

Hannah Smale (11)
Two Mile Hill Junior School

My Friend Katie

Always makes me laugh
One time she fell in the swimming bath
My friend Katie
Protects me from bad
When she hugs me I feel ever so glad
My friend Katie
Is never ever glum
According to her she never has a full tum
My friend Katie
Tells me right from wrong
Every day she sings a happy song
My friend Katie
Doesn't like school
She'd much rather dive in a swimming pool
My friend Katie
Never stops trying
Not in a million years would you catch her crying
My friend Katie
Is loaded with pranks
She is scared if I say spank
My friend Katie
Is very loveable indeed
When she wants something she has to plead
I like my friend Katie and always will forever.

Elsie Elder (9)
Two Mile Hill Junior School

A Frosty Winter

Winter is cold
Winter is damp
Winter is full of frost
Winter is all around the air
Winter cannot be sold.

Put on your mittens, put on your scarf
Don't forget your hat, then go outside and play around
And feel cold wherever you're at.

Scrunch some snow together, then roll it round and
Build it up until it's tall then squash it so it's flat.

When the sky begins to go dark
You go inside your house
Where there is no cold and it's just warm
And be silent as a mouse.

Now like I said before
Winter is cold and damp
But make the most of it while you can
Because it only comes once a year.

Winter is cold
Winter is damp
Winter is full of frost
Winter is all around the air
Winter cannot be sold.

Sarah Giddings (11)
Two Mile Hill Junior School

The School Sound Collector

(Inspired by 'The Sound Collector' by Roger McGough)

The tapping of the keyboard
The music of the hall
The munching of the lunches
The bouncing of balls
The scratching of the white boards
The ringing of the phones
The knocking of the doors
The praying of the Lord.

Jamie Coatsworth (9)
Two Mile Hill Junior School

Detention

As I walk through the door
My trainers squeak on the polished floor
Squirming in stomach's pit
The corridor dull and dimly lit
I gulp my lump out my throat
I wait to face my teacher gloat.

Gemma Challenger (10)
Weston Park Primary School

There Was An Old Lady

There was an old woman from Slough
Whose dog ran away with a cow
She ran down the street
With two fish on her feet
And knocked herself out with a plough.

Ceri-Mai Shepherd (10)
Weston Park Primary School

School

School dinners are very mouldy
My teacher is an oldy
Say hay hay
Say hay hay

As I stand in the line
I get a stupid fine
No no yeah
No no yeah

I'm Mr Rushtastic
He so fantastic
He's the best to cook
Even look at his recipe book
Say hay hay
Say hay hay

I'm at the front of the line
I'm waiting to dine
The food's in there
But I don't care
No no yeah
No no yeah.

Dale Hill (10)
Weston Park Primary School

Tsunami Disaster

Were they prepared . . . ? No
Did they see it coming . . . ? No

Devastation was caused
The reason . . . ? No one knows

The world unites as one
We give to those in need

We hope in time their wounds will heal
So they can get back on their feet.

Rebecca Jenkins (11)
Weston Park Primary School

School

Oh please, oh please don't give me detention
All I want is a little attention
I will not play in the mud
I promise I will be good
English, maths
I will take the right path
I will not lie
I will always try
I will behave in geography
And don't forget history
I will read every night
I will not get in a fight
I will help around the classroom more
I will not say this class is a bore
Colouring in
I will not throw others' work in the bin
So please don't give me detention
Also did I mention
I will help out at dinner time
I will not say everything is mine
One more thing
So ring-a-ding-ding
Pencil crayons blue and red
Finally I go to bed.

Katy Weech (9)
Weston Park Primary School

Full Moon

A white chocolate button going into a dark, dark mouth
The end of a torch shining in a pitch-black room
A rich tea biscuit going into a cup of black coffee.

Lauren Walker-Staynings (10)
Weston Park Primary School

True Love

I just couldn't live without you
You mean everything to me
I never realised how wonderful
Being in love could be

You showed me the secret
That turned my life around
In the time we've been together
True love I have found

You're the one person
I'll love my whole life through
Nothing will ever come before
This love I have for you

So promise me you'll always stay
In this heart of mine
And we will be the happiest
Till the end of time.

Charlotte Reed (10)
Weston Park Primary School

School

Detention was invented
For kids who are demented
The toilets are dinky
And they're really stinky

School dinners are so stale
And day after day they get pale
No one likes them
And will never ever bite them

We flick pencils, we flick pens
The teacher gets mad, and we get sad.

Luke Jones (10)
Weston Park Primary School

My Love

My love is like a rose
Blooming all the time
When people cuddle in the moonlight
It's like a clinging vine

Love is precious
To the heart
Love will never leave
It's for all to see

Love is a light
That brightens up the sky
Stars will light up the sky
But not like love.

Oliver Rush (10)
Weston Park Primary School

The Tsunami

The wave hit
No chance to run
The dead were buried in a pit
This was as bad as the Somme

Everyone scared
Trying to escape
Running wild
Fleeing for life's sake.

Daniel Jewell (11)
Weston Park Primary School

Child's Play

It's child's play so do a somersault
It's child's play to say it's not your fault
It's child's play to swim in the sea
And it's child's play to play with me!

Joseph Stewart (11)
Weston Park Primary School

House Noise

The squeaking of the birds
The dripping of the tap
The ticking of the clock
The crunching of my crisp
The clicking of the remote

The ring of the bell
The freezing of my drink
The burning of my toast
The slamming of the door
The barking of the dog

The scratching of the cat
The yacking of the parents
The nibbling of the rabbits
The snoring in my sleep
The sizzling of my sausages

The steaming of the kettle
The creaking of the floorboards
The hooting of the horn
The revving of the engine
And the whistling of the wind.

Jack Randall (10)
Weston Park Primary School

The Supply

I stumbled down the corridor
It was as dark as death with blue walls
I looked up through the skylight
As it was blurred by rain
We marched like soldiers into the room
Just about to meet our doom
Going out to play all day
Tomorrow will be another day.

Zachary Fredericks (11)
Weston Park Primary School

Hercules

Greece, Greece
I'm learning about Greece
It's really fun but
My best bit
It's the best
He's the best
The best
The almighty
The strong, brave
Hercules
The man as strong as an ox
As willing as a clown walking the tight rope
As strong as a bull trying to get out of jail
As brave as a lion
He's a hero
Do you know all of those labours he did?
Twelve of them
Amazing.

Hannah Weekes (9)
Weston Park Primary School

My Onomatopoeia Poem

The humming of the kettle
The tick-tock of the clock
The chattering of the plates
The clicking of the lock.

The ping of the microwave
The beeping of the alarm
The ding of the bell
As I hear the 'moo' from the farm.

Alex McGill (10)
Weston Park Primary School

Valentine's Day

Love is spread around
Till it falls on the ground
You get sweets
And lots of other treats
You'll find your true love
He will send you a white dove
Champagne, sparkle and bubbles
Soothing all your troubles
Shiny, sparkling dust
Cupid's arrows are a must
Making people fall in love
When he shoots them from above
So when I ask you to be my valentine
Please say that you will be mine.

Kara Houson (9)
Weston Park Primary School

Teardrop

They are at it again
Squeezing through my eyelids
Like wind and rain
I try to put on a brave face
But all of the things
I can't rest my case
All of the things buzzing around in my mind
Looking for closure, I cannot find
I wipe my eyes, so no one can see
The things I feel inside of me.

Molly Scull (10)
Weston Park Primary School

Noises At Night

The whistling of the kettle
The dripping of the taps
The buzzing of the freezer
The spitting of the fat

The creaking of the floorboards
The banging of the doors
The cracking of the fire
Is someone walking on my floor?

My knees begin to wobble
My legs begin to shake
I hope I get to sleep tonight
But I'll probably stay awake.

Deakon Richards (10)
Weston Park Primary School

The Playground

People starting fights
Tripping over laces
Running on the concrete
Crashing into bins
Children buying fruit
Sprinting on the field
Kicking the ball at the wall
Playing basketball
Skipping rope

This, my friends
Is the playground
We would not have it any other way.

Jack Finney (11)
Weston Park Primary School

The Tsunami Disaster

People try to run and hide from this creature so alive
Woosh, crash, bang, smash
Ruining everything in its path

The earth has moved and families lost
This tragedy will never be forgotten

The water has subsided
The crying now stopped
All people come together
To build new houses and shops

The world knows that these are dark days
But tourists will return for their holidays
People around the world are still giving
And families are making a new home to live in.

Sophie Wheeler (10)
Weston Park Primary School

Terror Of The Second World War

Rockets whistling
Bullets flying
People screaming
All around
Soldiers dying
Bombs dropping
Sirens going up and down

Planes flying overhead
Fighting as they go
People hiding under stairs
It's the worst war
In 21 years.

Jamie Hawkins (10)
Weston Park Primary School

The Family From Brass

There was an old lady from Brass
She always chewed on grass
Her husband was mouldy
Her sister was baldy
This isn't the end of the story
She always stole other people's glory
Her daughter had big feet
Her son always said 'Tweet'
Her dad always liked to bet
Her mum always seemed upset
Her uncle was dead
Her aunt always stayed in bed
And I think that's where I need to go.

Reece Godfrey (11)
Weston Park Primary School

Inside The House

The splashing of the water
The banging of the doors
The dripping of the tap
The clicking of the clock

The humming of the heater
The shushing of the cooker
The clashing of the cutlery
The begging at your door.

Amy Hart (11)
Weston Park Primary School

I Wanna Be

I wanna be a soldier
When I am older
I wanna drive an army tank
My shots will be point blank

I want to pilot a big plane
But I don't want all the strain
I want this job to work
I won't act like a jerk.

Ewan Estcourt (9)
Weston Park Primary School

Seabed

Cool and calm
Under the seabed
Where some swimmers have swam
Fishes and crab
Mermaids are fab
Under the seabed.

Gemma Chandler (11)
Weston Park Primary School